SISTERS ON SISTERS

SISTERS ON SISTERS

JANE DOWDESWELL

with Foreword by Katie Boyle

GRAPEVINE

First published 1988

British Library Cataloguing in Publication Data

Dowdeswell, Jane
Sisters on sisters.
1. Sisters
I. Title
308.8'754

ISBN 0-7225-1397-6

Grapevine is an imprint of the Thorsons Publishing Group,
Wellingborough, Northampton, NN8 2RQ, England

Printed in Great Britain by Woolnough Bookbinding Limited
Irthlingborough, Northamptonshire

1 3 5 7 9 10 8 6 4 2

CONTENTS

To three special sisters —
Florence, Mildred and Lilian Price.

FOREWORD

There's no doubt in my mind, from very personal experience, that blood is definitely thicker than water — Jane Dowdeswell's book has confirmed my convictions.

The endless and very individual permutations of emotions that go hand in hand with sisterhood are all here in *Sisters on Sisters* . They will certainly strike many a chord in us all.

I had 23 years as an only child, and can say, with hand on heart, that I much prefer this big wide world now that I know that my half sister Margherita is around to turn to if I need her.

This is a very well observed and reported book which confirms the many advantages and just the very few disadvantages of being, and having, a sister.

Katie Boyle
London
1988

INTRODUCTION

'Sisters? A book about sisters? What about them? Either you've got one or you haven't.' That's the reaction of some people when I first mention this book, but go a little deeper and sisterhood is one of the most complex, rewarding relationships.

It hasn't been analysed like the relationships with parents or partners. Indeed, if we believed the media we would think the only significant relationship in our lives is a romantic one. Yet sisterhood is probably the one that will last longer than any other. One woman said, a husband comes and goes, but a sister will always be around. She is someone to look up to, not for shallow reasons, like worldly success, but for their sensitivity and sensibility.

If you have sisters, you probably haven't put your feelings for each other into words — apart from in the heat of an argument! Writing this book certainly prompted me to find out my sister's first memories of me. I'd learnt of the violent impact a younger sister's arrival can have from others, but had she resented me when I came along to take my place in *her* world? No, for her my arrival was greeted with curiosity. She recalls her first vision 'through the cot bars, a miniature me asleep?' But growing more cautious of the strange screaming and waving arms she came closer, only to be dragged off by mum yet again. Hearing, too, that the way sisters play together hints at how their relationship will develop, I was intrigued to recall our own playtimes. Okay so we weren't like the Brontës who had their miniature world of toy soldiers and fantasy islands, or the Mitfords with their secret language, but we had something far better — our Sindy dolls. Susan would always far rather have my dolls than her own, which I discover is a characteristic of many sisters, including Princess

Grace who always played with her sisters' dolls, keeping her own in tip top condition.

My own sister remembers us 'making houses across the entire floor, mine soon untidy and abandoned, Jane still organizing with military precision, insisted on laying Sindy's table for dinner — down to the last spoon.' From childhood to adulthood our story is much the same: I 'good at organizing, and preaching practicalities and good sense' (so she says!). She full of enviable dreams and illusions. We are so different, yet shared so much, a closeness, yet a distance.

I was the one always saying, 'Me too', demanding, or sometimes begging, to be included in her games. In this I am like so many younger sisters, including one, Margaret, who would chase her older sister on her tricycle along the passageways of their home shouting out 'Wait for me, Lilibet, wait for me!' Lilibet, is in fact, Queen Elizabeth, and the home none other than Buckingham Palace!

Childhood memories are most precious, the starting point for a sisterly relationship that's set on a course of ups and downs. Sisters can be responsible for so many things: making you laugh, making you mad, stealing your first boyfriend, giving you your first niece. Part of you always pulling back in a desire to be your own person, the rest of you needing to be close and nurturing the exclusive sense of security. A sister is someone who has reason to be very much like you, but she can also be your deepest adversary.

This book may contain a slightly biased view of sisterhood: certainly there can be great bitterness and jealousy between sisters, but most of the women who relished talking about sisterhood were those who most treasured it. I have felt a part of so many sisters' lives, women who let me share their most precious memories, in particular, Pat Bradford who loved and lost her sister Sue during the course of writing this book. My thanks also go to Deirdre who gave me countless leads on fascinating sisters, to Michelle, Gill Plain, and to Shirley Dunmall and Rebecca Leathlean who helped me with the endless number of interviews. And, of course, to my parents who have been responsible for so many things, but perhaps most significantly they ensured I had a sister of my very own.

Jane Dowdeswell
London
1988

Jane Dowdeswell and her elder sister.

Chapter 1

My Sister

WHAT WOULD WE DO WITHOUT OUR SISTER? SISTERLY TIES ARE SPECIAL, BUT HOW AND WHY?

MY SISTER IS. . .

. . . my rock—I could never find a friend who would give so much.

Jessica Martin, 25

. . .the person I want to be. She has my strengths but not my weaknesses.

Louise, 20

. . .the only person I'd give my last Rolo to.

Hannah, 23

. . .dependent on me, and I wouldn't want it any other way.

Jayne Irving, 31

. . .someone to borrow clothes from.

Jodi, 22

. . .a nuisance. She always wants to tag along and play with my friends.

Emma, 12

. . .my confidante, my best friend, my ally.

Julie, 32

. . . my memory—she brings back to life all our happy childhood days, she makes me feel secure.

Mary, 76

. . . a stranger, someone who knows a lot about me, and yet I know nothing about her.

Sinitta, 21

. . . the one person who tolerated me, defended me, played with me, whereas friends are often 'fair weather' friends. She was always there.

Sylvia, 63

. . . like a best friend you can't get rid of. You know that whatever you do, they'll still be there.

Amy Li, 30

. . . somebody else to turn to apart from Mum, and someone I can talk to about subjects Mum and I can't talk about.

Harriet, 13

. . . GREAT!

Emily, 5

Emily probably sums up in one word what a lot of sisters feel. If you have a sister, how difficult do you find it to put into words your feelings for her? Whether you love her or hate her, your sister arouses strong emotions. Few other relationships can inspire such loyalty or such anger. Sisters can experience great closeness, but when they fall out, the conflicts go deeper, too.

One woman said, 'When I'm happy, I feel guilty if she isn't. If she's on top of the world and everything's going badly for me, I feel resentful.'

MORE THAN A FRIEND

Your sister is also the one person you will probably know for longer than any other. Whether that is as your strength, a lifeline, a best friend, or as your biggest enemy depends on the sister! When you're growing up, a sister can be a readymade playmate; as a teenager, you've got a live-in counsellor, as a mother, you've got an automatic auntie and willing babysitter, in old age, you've got someone who doesn't get bored by all your stories of the 'good old days'. But beware: that playmate can so easily turn into an enemy, your teenage counsellor into a live-in rival.

Perhaps you have more reason to love your sister of all people because you share so much. But you have much reason to dislike her too: you occupy each other's lives for many years, and every way you turn she is there competing with you for all you hold dear. As one sister said, 'I wouldn't choose her, but I wouldn't want to lose her.' On the one hand you want to be close, on the other you feel threatened by losing your identity. It is the most complex relationship central to women's lives, yet few people have analysed it in the way marriage or motherhood have been scrutinized. There is an underlying bond between sisters, even among those who claim not to get on. Says one sister: 'I think it's a myth that because you're related you should like each other and get on, but for some reason you feel obliged to do so.'

Some sisters believe that to confess to outsiders that you have anything but a close relationship sounds at worst like a betrayal, at best unnatural. *Others* say it's okay for sisters to criticize each other—you're only human, after all! But *all* sisters appear to agree that if one of them hears a bad word about the other, they will defend them to the end: a sister will bail you out without question, guilty or not guilty.

Jodi Knight says of her oldest sister: 'I would really lay into anyone who said anything horrible about Abby,' and Abby counters: 'Jodi is the only person I would lie for to get her out of trouble.'

Other sisters have said much the same:

> I would support my sister to the end. Even if she committed murder, I would stand by her. I would tell her she was crazy, but to the outside world I would defend her all the way. To do otherwise would be to betray the bond between you. I feel that about my sister more than I do for my parents or my brother.
>
> *Jo*

> Perhaps there is a morality in having a sister that is not there with a best friend, or anyone else. I'd probably find myself defending Harriet for things I morally disagree with. In fact, I'd probably defend Harriet better than I could defend myself.
>
> *Becky*

Carol Hayes, one of four sisters, says, 'If one of my sisters was up for murder it goes without saying that I'd defend them, but don't ask me to live with them,' and that probably sums up how a lot of sisters feel. 'It's blood—family is family, and she's my sister. But don't ask me to be her friend, too!'

BEING THERE FOR EACH OTHER

A sister will always be there to defend, protect and just 'help out'. When Lena Zavaroni fell victim to anorexia nervosa, it was her younger sister who protected her from the unwanted attention of the press. Look at news cuttings of the time and it is Carla, two years younger than Lena, who is there helping to fend off the questions.

Emma Samms, who played Fallon in *The Colbys* and *Dynasty*, also knows the value of sisterhood. She and her sister Louise grew up in Harrow, Middlesex, and when she became successful she needed someone to run her fan club. Who better than her sister? It was certainly not an easy job, for along with John James, it was Emma who got the most fan mail. Fortunately, her sister now lives in Los Angeles, close by Emma and the studio.

Sarah Keays's two sisters have helped *her* through difficult times. When criticism was thrown at her for writing about her experiences with Cecil Parkinson, in *A Question of Judgement*, her younger sister Flora was the one who countered the criticism, claiming that they had shared 'a deep, meaningful relationship and not a cheap flimsy affair' as had been suggested. Read the book, and you feel envious of the sisterly closeness that clearly exists between Sarah, her twin Elizabeth, and Flora—a closeness which started in childhood, continued through schooldays and is as strong as ever today.

In *A Question of Judgement* Sarah writes of the pressures on her when the story first broke, and it is evident that she confided completely in her sisters, who helped her through a difficult time. Later it was her two sisters who were on either side of her when she gave birth to her daughter. It is hardly surprising that she called her Flora Elizabeth.

'Good' sisters should always cover each other. Jackie Collins says she was livid when her sister Joan didn't warn her that their mother had found her diary. They were both teenagers at the time, and the diary contained details of how she sneaked out when her parents thought she was tucked up in bed!

Another sister recalls:

> Our father was strict, so if we had been out with boyfriends we would arrange to meet at a certain time before coming home. Then we'd all stick to the same story—that we'd been to a dance together.
>
> *Anne*

But having a happy relationship with your sister doesn't mean there are never rows or disagreements, but, at the end of the day, you're still sisters. As Jessica Martin, comedienne and impersonator on *Spitting Image* and *Copycats* says:

> It's not always a bed of roses. We live together and usually it's great, but we have days when we have blazing arguments, too. On one occasion I said to Marianna to pack her bags, and she stormed

off. Then I sat down, expecting to feel relief, and instead I just thought 'Oh', and felt quite lost and really sorry. I know I'd be absolutely lost without my sister. She felt the same and came back!

SHARING THE LITTLE THINGS

Sisterhood isn't all about great 'highs' of intensity, or shows of emotion; often it's just feeling comfortable:

> When I want to flop down and not be on my own, I know I can sit with them and be fed up. When I need to run away from London, Hilary will pay for my return fare. If I didn't have my sisters, I know I'd be really miserable—friends only go so far.
>
> *Lucy*

Katie Boyle talks of her half sister, Margherita:

> She is 23 years younger than me; we have the same fathers, but different mothers. She calls me 'Eiderdown' because I'm comfortable! Having a sister means there is always someone who belongs—it is blood, a very special relationship.

Abby and Jodi Knight are two very close sisters, both in their twenties. Abby says having a sister is:

> Having a best friend, even if you're being stupid about something. You can get away with more with a sister than with a friend.

Jodi agrees:

> You can tell your sister really awful things and she'll still talk to you—we call it info-trading. You can be totally honest without falling out. We have counselling sessions in the bathroom. If one of us is in the bath, the other will come and sit and we'll chat over problems. I will always tell Abby the truth, even awful things, even if I know it might hurt her. I think it's better if she knows the truth about things, because I don't like people making a fool of her. I really love Abby and I hate it when friends say they hate their sisters. I can't understand it at all. I think they're missing out on such a lot. You can change a boyfriend every week, can't you, but you can't change your sister.

Susan Voak shares their view:

> I have two older sisters, and they are always there for me. Friends you can lose, but a sister you never will. It's different to having a

friend anyway. I tell my sister things I wouldn't tell a friend. Her opinions matter to me. If a friend said I was stupid for some reason or other I wouldn't take any notice, but if my sister said it, I would be really upset.

Some sisters say that they can't be anything *but* honest with each other.

My sister understands me a little too well. I can't fool her, pull the wool over her eyes. She always sees straight through me, so there's little option but to be totally honest with each other.

Deborah

Honesty is essential where sisters have gone into business together. Like Amy and Grace Li, two Chinese sisters originally from Hong Kong who run their own design company. Says Amy:

Having a sister is like having a best friend you can't get rid of. You know that whatever you do, they'll still be there. We work together as a partnership, and pull together. You know she won't sabotage the company or run off with all the money. Whatever happens, though, even if the partnership should fail, we'll still be sisters. It's easy enough to share a flat with a friend, but working with them? I wouldn't want to try that!

They recall the journalist who met them and said of the duo: 'It's impossible to talk about Amy without mentioning Grace—or Grace without mentioning Amy—in much the same way as you'd never say Rolls without tagging on Royce.' And, add Grace and Amy, they're sure it's their parents who have encouraged such closeness.

It is often the expectations of parents that encourage—and sometimes demand—closeness between sisters:

Mum had always said, 'Of course she will do it for you—she's your sister, isn't she?' I've never felt that my sisters are doing me a favour if I ask them something. It's just accepted in our family that you help each other.

Bonnie Langford says her parents brought all three sisters up to be a united family and now they know they can still rely on each other:

The other day I locked myself out of the house and I only had about half an hour before I had to leave for the show. I rang both my sisters and got through to Cherida and she came round straight away with another set of keys. They're always there to help me if I'm in any trouble. People say we all sound alike on the phone—

20

sometimes that's very useful. But when I phone Mummy I say, 'It's me,' and she will say, 'Which me?'

Another sister recalls how her mother brought her up to expect her older sisters to support her:

When I got married I had them both as bridesmaids. Shirley was a bit hesitant, she said she was too old, and I said, 'But you're my sister!' That's all it took—she did it.

Dawn

June Brown, who plays Dot Cotton in *EastEnders*, has always encouraged her four daughters to be close. June's older sister died from meningitis when she was just seven, and it made a lasting impression on her. She died in May and young June thought she'd be back for Christmas. When she didn't return she was desolate. Now she finds great security in her two younger sisters, who live close by and whom she sees regularly. Her four daughters, Louise, Sophie, Chloe and Naomi all follow separate careers but gather for a sisterly chat at mum's house at weekends.

Certainly in the past, it was assumed something was wrong with you if you didn't get on with your sisters—if you're not friends with your sisters, who can you be friends with?

It was just taken for granted in our family that you loved one another. You were thought to be the odd one out if you didn't love your sister. We shared a bedroom until she married—even the bed! In those days sisters often did—perhaps it was to do with lack of space. I don't know that sisters are encouraged to be so close nowadays. I see sisters who say they hate one another and I just can't understand that.

Sylvia

Becky Howard has three younger half-sisters, Harriet, Rosa and Ellen:

Having been an only daughter, and then suddenly finding myself with sisters gives me an incredible feeling of security in that I've got women who are going to be there for the rest of my life.

WE GET ON, BUT WE'RE VERY DIFFERENT

Have changing aspirations and lifestyles affected relationships between sisters? *Daily Mirror* Agony Aunt, Marje Proops, believes they have. From the letters she receives from sisters she is sure the same rivalries continue over men (and the race to get married which she experienced with

her only sister), but now there is the added competition caused by the ambition to succeed at a career, too. She believes the family structure has changed—and it is true, many sisters look outside the family for support, whereas once it was blood relations who were seen to 'rally round', particularly in large pre-war families.

One sister tells her story:

I was one of a family of eight children: five boys and three girls. When I was a little girl it was my brothers that I used to play with—one a little older and one a year younger than me. George (the younger one) and I were often taken for twins—like 'two peas in a pod'. We would play ball games like cricket and I remember them more as my playmates than my sisters, one of whom was three years older than me and the other two years younger.

But we were a very happy family and I remember I used to feel sorry for my little school friend, Babs Lee, who was an only child. I couldn't really imagine what life must have been like for her. My mother died when I was 14 and all our lives were sorely affected. My older sister became the 'mother' in the family and looked after my younger brothers. Life was really so different for us all.

Both of my sisters went to 'live-in' jobs and so we didn't see a great deal of one another in our teens and twenties. As each of us married and had children so we came together again, sharing one another's worries and joys. We didn't live close to one another but we would write to each other and occasionally see one another.

When the war came all the family split up. My brothers went into the Forces and I was the only one living in London, with my husband and little girl.

In the weeks leading up to the outbreak of war, there was an uneasy feeling of the inevitable: my eldest sister wrote to me, 'You must leave London and bring Maureen here to stay with us. It's not safe for you to stay in London.' This was my sister who already had a family of four children to feed and house, but who would make room for us in her small house away from the threat of bombing. I tried to thank her but she wouldn't have it. 'We're all one family and we must stick together.' I have often thought of her kindness—and her husband's—she just took us in with no thought of the inconvenience it must have caused them. That is what makes a sister so special—I don't think there is any other relationship quite like it.

Left Marje Proops and her younger sister.

SISTERS IN LITERATURE

For a relationship which is so central to women's lives it is curious that there is so little evidence of it in literature. Female writers have always tended to shy away from expressing feelings of love for another woman.

In Jane Austen's three most famous books: *Pride and Prejudice, Sense and Sensibility,* and *Mansfield Park,* sisters play a central role but it is often their relationship with prospective suitors rather than each other which receive most attention.

Jane Austen was one of eight children. She was said to be closest to her sister Cassandra, who was three years her elder. Indeed, their mother once commented that they copied each other to such a degree that, 'if Cassandra was going to have her head cut off, Jane would insist on sharing her fate.'

The two girls were sent away to school together and spent five years at Oxford and Reading. They became lifelong companions and always confided in each other.

Then Jane's health began to deteriorate. A mysterious illness gradually sapped all her strength and on 18 July 1817, she died in the arms of her sister, with whom she had shared her most intimate thoughts.

Envy is one of the many emotions women have expressed when they talk or write about their sisters. Virginia Woolf felt deeply inferior when her older sister, Vanessa, had children. Yet for Virginia, who was childless, it was less a feeling of envy, and more a sense of failure. She wrote in her diary: 'God, I wish I were dead. Pause. But why am I feeling this? Let me watch the wave rise. I watch. Vanessa. Children. Failure. Yes; I detect that. Failure, failure.'

Quentin Bell, who has written a biography of Virginia Woolf, concludes: 'It was to be a permanent source of grief to her and, in later years, she could never think of Vanessa's fruitful state without misery and envy.'

Yet despite this, Virginia and Vanessa were the closest of sisters and they found it difficult to accept that marriage could divide their loyalty to each other. 'Neither sister could really think that anyone was quite good enough for the other,' writes Quentin Bell. '. . . And if there were a difference of opinion between Vanessa and Leonard (Virginia's husband), Virginia would side with her husband. Marriage, so Vanessa discovered, had made Virginia a part of an alliance.'

These feelings are commonplace where sisters, especially twins, have shared a very close partnership. It can also cause problems in the marriage itself, and various studies have looked at the reasons for this. It seems that women who have been part of a 'pair' through sisterhood, and have experienced a particularly close and loving relationship, may have higher expectations of married life. You might enjoy a marvellous, almost telepathic relationship with a sister, and expect the same, if not more, from a marriage partner. However, for Virginia and Vanessa, it was the threat to their relationship which appeared to concern them most.

LITERARY SISTERS

Perhaps of all literary sisters it is the Brontës whose relationship has been most chronicled and analysed. Their closeness was encouraged by their mother, whose sister, Elizabeth, was also supportive. She came from Cornwall to nurse Mrs Brontë when she fell ill. When Mrs Brontë died it went without saying that, as her sister, Elizabeth would stay on and look after the children who came to call her Aunt Bramwell.

One of the daughters, Charlotte, seems to have based Jane Eyre's experiences at Lowood on her schooldays at Cowan Bridge School. Her two older sisters, Maria and Elizabeth, had only recently recovered from measles and whooping cough when they went to Cowan Bridge. The school was very cold and both daughters developed tuberculosis and died the following year. Their father removed Charlotte and Emily from the school, but the character in Jane Eyre, called Helen Burns, who suffered from consumption was obviously based on her sisters' illness. Charlotte's sensitive writings about Helen's subsequent death and her hopes to meet her again one day obviously sprang from her devotion to her two sisters.

Sisterly love is also expressed by Elizabeth Barrett Browning, who was one of 11 children. Her favourite sister was Arabella, who was seven years younger than herself. In her diary she described Arabella as 'an interesting, intelligent, amiable, feeling girl. I should love her if even she were not my sister—and even if she did not love me.'

In large families like Elizabeth Barrett Browning's there is often one sister who is left out. In What Katy Did, Susan Coolidge tells the story of the Carr family. Katy was the eldest. Then came Clover and Elsie, and Joanna was the youngest of the girls

'Poor little Elsie was the "odd one" among the Carrs. She didn't seem to belong exactly to either the older or the younger children. the great desire and ambition of her heart was to be allowed to go about with Katy and Clover . . . But they didn't want Elsie, and used to tell her to "run away and play with the children." In almost every large family there is one of these left-out children.'

Daphne du Maurier was the middle sister of three. Her diaries, published as Myself When Young, record her happy childhood days, but even at

25

a young age, sisterly comparisons were evident: 'Both Jeanne and Angela were far more musical than I was. Angela had her voice "trained" and Jeanne already played the piano very well indeed, and showed promise at drawings and painting. My only talent seemed to be writing stories.'

Later these differences became more significant, puzzling Daphne, who wrote in her diary: 'Angela and Jeanne were content with their lives. Why did I have to be different? We three got on so well, we never quarrelled, and could discuss every subject under the sun; yet they had no desire to break away, as I did.'

By expressing these differences with her own sisters Daphne du Maurier touched on the one element of sisterhood which is most often highlighted in literature.

More recently, author and ex-model Pat Booth, described the physical differences between Jane and Julie, the two sisters who are the main characters in her book, *The Sisters*:

'The similarity could not be denied, but it was the differences that caught the attention. When the genetic cards had been dealt she had been left holding the nines and tens while the royal cards had gone to Jane. Julie's proportions were fine, but she was too damn big, and Jane, in contrast, so effortlessly "right". A sidelong glance at the mirror told the whole story.'

And in Helen Van Slyke's novel *Sisters and Strangers* three very different sisters meet up for the first time in 30 years for their parents' golden wedding anniversary. Fran, the eldest, is nine years older than Barbara, the 'baby', and Allie, the middle one, is a year younger than Fran. The story is woven around each of their lives since they left home to marry or embark on a career, and although each sister's pattern of life does not always meet with the others' approval, all would defend each other's right to choose.

Through the different crises which occur during their stay with their parents, it is to each other that they turn, sometimes in anger, but more often in despair, comforting and gaining strength from one another.

George Eliot was one of the earliest female authors to give credit to the strength and power of women's mutual love. In *Middlemarch*, the young Celia is always in the shadow of her more striking and clever sister, Dorothea. However, when she matures and becomes a mother she feels more able to advise her childless sister Dorothea and remarks that no one could understand and love Dodo so well as she did.

Male writers seem to fear this unity and strength in women's friendships. For example, Charles Dickens renders sisterhood powerless through petty jealousies and resentments. In *Little Dorrit*, the younger sister, Amy, assumes the responsibility of the older, washing and cleaning for Fanny. Their relationship becomes that of mother and daughter. Fanny is clearly jealous of Amy's virtues and that jealousy causes her to act erratically and unkindly. When she is criticized for being cruel to Amy she attempts to make amends but ends up awakening 'much affectionate uneasiness in her sister's mind that day by passing the greater part of it in violent fits of embracing her, and in alternately giving her brooches, and wishing herself dead.' In Dickens, sisterhood is never portrayed as a relationship that should be emulated or envied.

MORE SIMILARITIES THAN DIFFERENCES

Some literary sisters have found that despite differences there are advantages in having a sister. Recent examples of literary sisters include the Longford daughters, most notably Antonia Fraser and Rachel Billington; and the Drabbles: the novelist Margaret and her two sisters, A.S. Byatt and art historian Dr Helen Langdon.

Unlike the Brontës, Margaret has said that she and her sisters were not very close as children, and it was only during holidays that they spent a lot of time together. Perhaps, she suggests, that's why their books, like their adult names, are so different.

In the light of this it is interesting to read how Margaret Drabble touches on sisterhood in her novel *Jerusalem the Golden*. It is similarities, not differences, that her main character, Clara, resents. When she first meets Annunciata, the sister of her close friend, Clelia, she is disturbed by their likeness because she does not like to think 'that Clelia was in any way thinned or dispersed or diluted by such a close resemblance; she wanted her to be unique.'

Margaret Drabble superbly sums up the relationship between the two sisters: 'They displaced each other, they encouraged each other; they spoke about their impending, transient, trivial separation with real regret. They put their arms around each other; they laughed, in the same key, at each other's jokes.' It was all new to Clara, who had not seen such an open show of affection between sisters. She only knew that sisters could dislike and resent one another until they went their separate ways in marriage and motherhood:

'Her acquaintances in Northam, she thought, would have considered such affection unnatural, and probably perverted, if not wholly insincere, and there was something in herself that could not help but suspect it: and yet at the same time it seemed to absolve a whole area of human relationship, to rescue it, wholesale, from the scruffy ragbag of the tag ends of family bitterness and domestic conflict. And such affection had, surely, its precedents, for were not sisters classically intended to love, and not to despise one another?'

Margaret Drabble's reference to people who might find such open affection between sisters 'as unnatural, and probably perverted' is not extreme. It may also suggest why some earlier writers have been loathe to explore sisterhood in great depth—intimacy between women was not a subject for our Victorian brothers—or sisters.

Of course, it may simply be that writers did not value the bond between sisters as highly as the relationship between men and women. But despite this, the close relationship between sisters has become symbolic. The term sisterhood has been adopted by the women's movement and is applied to the closest of religious groups.

SPECIAL FRIENDS

Women who have not experienced life as a sister say they are envious of the sisterly relationships they have observed:

Although I had three brothers, I always wanted a sister. I love my brothers dearly, but there is not that bond which I'm sure exists between sisters and which would be so special to me now.

Anne

I was an only child, and I suppose I've always gone out of my way to make close friends. In fact, I had one girl friend who lived in London in a flat we shared for five years and people used to think we were sisters. I liked that.

Linda

I was an only child and I didn't seem to mind when I was younger— all my friends seemed to be only children, we were all born in the depression of the 1930s.

When I was 11 I was evacuated and lived in a large house with 36 other girls. It was run on boarding school lines. I was there until I was 14 and I suppose it was like having sisters. But now I'm older and both of my parents have died I would dearly love to have a sister—someone to talk to about childhood days and shared memories. I have a good husband and two daughters, but a sister would be so very special.

Kathy

I realized it was something special to have a sister when I started secondary school. It was a really tough place, and the younger girls used to get picked on—all except three girls in the class who had sisters in the fifth year. I knew then it must be a big advantage to have an older sister!

Marilyn

Older or younger, despite differences and distances, a sister is always there:

Although we live miles apart, we're like best friends and it's just like yesterday when we all get together—it's as if we've never been apart. Even when we don't see each other for ages, news travels really fast between us—it's a race to see who can get on the phone first to pass on the news. My sisters are like Indians—they sit on top of mountains and give out smoke signals!

Lucinda

Alison describes the relationship with her three sisters as a network:

The great thing with sisters is that you can always get news to travel fast! Although our lifestyles are quite different, we are all openly and demonstrably supportive of each other. I can't imagine life without sisters.

Ivy Spender, an only child, is the mother of Lynne and Dale Spender (who had their letters to each other published in the book *Scribbling Sisters*). She was delighted when her second daughter, Lynne, was born. 'The greatest gift I have given is each to the other,' she remarked.
In the foreword to their book she writes:

Not having a sister myself, I daydreamed about each of them having a constant companion through life, always able to enjoy things together. In their early years there were times when there was little togetherness, but let any other person criticize or oppose either one in any way and they became as inseparable as Siamese twins!

SHE IS MY SISTER, AFTER ALL

Outsiders can't always appreciate the strength of feeling between sisters. One woman says it's a constant source of conflict between her boyfriend and herself:

He says I do too much for my sister and that I get nothing back in return. But he doesn't understand—I don't want any reward— she's my sister.

Joanne

Julie's youngest sister lives in Manchester, where she's been blacklisted for not paying bills, has taken an overdose, is out of work and has started to steal. Julie's boyfriend hardly speaks to her sister and says she is a 'waste of space', but Julie says she could never turn her back on her:

I found it difficult to tell her how I felt, so I wrote a letter to her. I remember there used to be some good times, and I want to help her. When I see her I try to imagine what she's going through. I found myself giving her money last time I was with her. I feel so responsible as the oldest—she is such a significant part of my life. But my boyfriend thinks I'm far too involved. He once said he hoped I'll put him first when we get married.

It was the Beverley Sisters who put into words the torn loyalties between sisters and their men. But Babs, Teddie and Joy have never had the same problems over their loyalties to each other: 'We may be stars to the world, but we are not stars to one another. We are just sisters,' they said at the height of their fame. 'One will make quite clear to the other two that they cannot be stars on their own. One Beverley Sister is useless. Two Beverley Sisters are useless. Only three Beverley Sisters are stars. Divided—we fall.'

Other sisters who have gone on to great success include the Nolans, the Irish family who started out as 'eight sisters, two brothers, Mum, Dad, cat and kitchen sink,' over 20 years ago. The brothers and parents dropped out, and two of the sisters left to follow solo careers, but the Nolans are still going strong.

Mel and Kim have been even more successful as singing sisters. Nick East, boss at Supreme Records, recalls how he had been looking for two stunning black singers for a song he'd already lined up. Mel and Kim fitted the bill perfectly—and the fact that they were sisters certainly added to their appeal. Behind the scenes the sisters' success is carefully engineered: differences are minimized with identical clothes and clever camera angles; and it's always Mel on the left, Kim on the right—on records, in headlines, in photographs.

When it comes to spotting the oldest and youngest sisters in a family, some people say you can instantly tell who is who: the younger anxious for recognition, the older effortlessly superior. An American psychologist, Dr Kevin Leman, believes that family order can shape your destiny, and has a lasting influence on your characters and achievements. He reports that first-born sisters, like only children, tend to be perfectionists, always in control of their lives. Middle-borns have to struggle for a share of attention and by so doing develop individual characters. The youngest sister is often the under-achiever. She has an easy ride through childhood having been generally spoilt and indulged.

Julie Siegar, the youngest of five sisters says:

I suppose I was most spoilt. They all had to wait longer for things whereas I got everything at a young age. For instance, they all had to wait till they were 21 for the gold bracelet. I was still in my teens when I got one. But then, I'm forever saying 'My sister did . . .' or 'My sister says . . .' and in a way you feel quite knowledgeable even though you haven't really experienced very much yourself. Some may say that this is why younger sisters tend to achieve less.

Of all the comments made by psychologists, there is one, in particular, few sisters would dispute: that the 'baby' sister stays just that all her life. Lady Sarah, the eldest sister of the Princess of Wales, said of Diana: 'I'm sure it won't change Diana in any way. For me she will always remain my sweet, lovable little sister.'

Evidently there are very few things that can come between sisters.

Chapter 2

ALLIES AND RIVALS

WHAT MAKES GOOD SISTERS? HOW IMPORTANT IS THE AGE
DIFFERENCE? WHAT IS IT LIKE BEING THE ELDER OR YOUNGER SISTER?

THE NEW ARRIVAL

Can you remember the first time you became aware that you had a sister? Probably not — it doesn't quite happen like that. If you're the youngest, your sister has always been there. If you're the oldest you might
remember the sudden arrival of your sister, and those equally sudden
feelings of resentment, jealousy or excitement.

Older sisters tend to express more hostility than younger ones: 'Why
did she have to come along and mess everything up?' asked one six-year-
old, which probably sums up a what a lot of sisters haven't put into words.
But the earliest feelings are often excitement and puzzlement. Kim
Appleby, of singing duo Mel and Kim, says her first impression of Mel
was that she had strange hands:

> She was born with twelve fingers, like our dad — it's quite com-
> mon in Jamaica, But I was 5 at the time and I was fascinated. They
> cut off the extra two when she was still a baby.

Cherida Langford, eldest sister of Bonnie, also a successful dancer, can
remember waiting at the hospital with her dad and younger sister Pet,
anxious for news of the next family arrival: 'Suddenly the nurse dashed
out with a tiny bundle and we all adored her from then on.'

Barbara Woodhouse, in her autobiography *Just Barbara*, says that the
very first incident she can remember with any clarity is the birth of her

sister, Hazel. Barbara was just 18 months at the time and recalls: 'On peeping closer I saw a mass of straight black hair surrounding a tiny little face; she was fast asleep'. She was told she could only look but not touch this new novelty in the family. She soon lost interest: it seemed 'an awfully dull thing to do with a new sister', and instead of wanting to play she just made 'horrible screaming noises'. Barbara blames her early dislike of babies on this experience; even at that early age she says she preferred animals!

Pat Bradford was eight when her baby sister Susan was born. But they were miles apart, as it was wartime and Pat had been evacuated to Cornwall:

> I'll always remember when I first set eyes on her. She had these strange tufts of red hair, and she had measles. I had never seen such a strange looking thing in all my life!

Princess Caroline of Monaco remembers that February 1, 1965 was a very special day for her. It was the birth of her younger sister Stephanie, and it prompted her to say: 'This is the most beautiful day of my life'. Almost immediately she wanted to take her to school and show her off to all her friends!

Willi Frischauer, writing a biography of Jackie (Bouvier Kennedy) Onassis, records the day before the inauguration of President Roosevelt on March 3 1933. To Jackie, not yet four, it was significant for the arrival of another 'doll' — a live doll — to add to her collection. Unlike many older sisters she seemed unperturbed by the arrival of her younger sister Caroline, who became known as Lee: 'Jackie looked poised and self assured as she posed by the side of Lee's crib and contemplated the newcomer with quizzical eyes. She clearly did not begrudge the baby a share of mother's studied, clinical but still generous affection'.

Jean is 12 years older than her sister Marie and, like Jackie Onassis, remembers it was like suddenly having one of *her* dolls come to life:

> I used to take her out and push her about in the pram. I loved it — she was a real live doll for me. Because she was so much younger I used to want to help dress her, and feed her. All my other dolls were left to fend for themselves.

No-one can be 100 per cent sure how age difference affects the sisterly relationship. Some believe the closer the gap, the closer the relationship. However, studies show that personality and the relationship with parents have far greater importance to the quality of the sisterly bond.

Despite this, most parents 'plan' families with age gaps in mind (the

The Princesses Caroline and Stephanie (Courtesy Keystone Collection).

most common being 2-3 years) and are increasingly aware of the potential jealousies that can explode when the new sibling arrives.

WHY DID I HAVE TO HAVE A SISTER?

However hard parents try to include the elder at the birth of younger sisters, it seems almost inevitable that the first child will experience a loss in attention when the second child comes along. Child psychologists have also found that mothers do tend to 'champion' the younger sister, i.e. 'she can hit me, but I can't hit her back', and the first-born is convinced they get far more of the blame. Certainly when parents are prepared to take sides it appears to instigate further quarrelling and rivalry, rather than resolve the argument!

Judy Dunn, a child psychologist who has conducted major studies into sibling relationships, points out that sisters don't choose each other, so we shouldn't be amazed that they don't always get on when forced to live in 'daily, and intense intimacy'. The assumption has always been that if we're *born* of the same parents then there should be likenesses. And indeed it is true that siblings are *more* genetically similar to each other than they are to their parents. But the fact that we have 50 per cent of genes in common with our sisters means we can be as *disalike* as we are alike. And those genes we do share influence physical traits, such as colouring and height, far more than personality. So the differences should surprise no-one.

Parents should not feel they have failed in any way if there is conflict between sisters; nor should they force them to get on. One woman, recalling her childhood, says she is sure she and her sister would have been good friends if they hadn't been forced upon each other so much. Their parents insisted they spent every minute together:

> It wasn't enough that we liked each other reasonably well — it was expected of us to love each other deeply. We ended up bitterly jealous and almost hating one another.

Even jealousy is said to be an expression of how much we mean to each other. But some research suggests there is far less jealousy between sisters than there is between a brother and sister. Perhaps this is because we find more in common with a sister, or because same-sex children are treated more similarly by parents.

Although the sense of rivalry may not be so acute, the comparisons thrive from cot to classroom, and further: the proud grandmother in the maternity ward is often heard saying: 'She's so different from her older sister — she's such a quiet little thing and so good'. Most families have 'the good sister' and 'the bad one', 'the pretty one' and the 'clever one'. The eldest one is often categorized as the dutiful one, while the younger is often the rebellious, frivolous sister. As sisters grow up this can result in intense dislike of each other: for instance the pretty one becomes convinced she must, by default, be brainless.

Whereas we choose our friends — by their interests and characters — we have no say in the kind of sister we get. Julie Marshall remembers her childhood with younger sister Samantha:

> I didn't get on with Samantha at all; we looked different, we liked different games, and we had nothing in common. Mum used to say the hospital must have given her the wrong baby — it was impossible for two sisters to be so unalike!

When singer Sinitta met her twin sister for the first time after growing up apart, everyone, herself included had great expectations:

We're twins, we're both girls, what more could we have in common? You just assume you'll get on. But we couldn't have been more different. She was just not the kind of person I would choose for a friend under normal circumstances.

Carol Hayes, who now runs a successful public relations company in London, says she and her three sisters are all very different, and when they were younger none of them got on well:

Natalie was the oldest and she used to think we were really silly. We were always fighting even when we played. Like we'd play 'cowboys and Indians', and they'd throw me on my dad when he was asleep in the chair. I think it's too much to expect four individuals, like we were, to hit it off. I don't know how dad coped either, with five women. I was always the small one, and felt I had to make the loudest noises. I didn't realize it then but I think I wanted attention.

DADDY'S GIRL

The arrival of a younger sister is sometimes seen as a kind of dethronement. Joan Collins had been her father's 'angel'; for the first five years of her life she had him all to herself. Then along came Jackie. In her autobiography *Past Imperfect* Joan Collins writes: 'I can't pinpoint exactly when I stopped being daddy's little darling. It could have been when little baby Jackie arrived to take some of the attention away from me.'

Many older sisters remember how they developed close relationships with their fathers when mum was suddenly too busy with the new arrival to spend much time with them. One woman talks about that moment in her life:

I'd always wanted to be with mum much more than with dad — he was always at work anyway. When Pauline came along mum didn't have as much time for me, and I wanted to make mum jealous. She had Pauline, and I wanted her to know I had someone else — my dad. Ever since then I've been known as daddy's girl, and he calls me his little princess.

A younger sister puts a different perspective on the course of events:

I think it must be really difficult if you're the older sister and suddenly this baby comes along taking up all your mother's time and attention. My sister was only two when I was born, but in fact she stayed closest to my mother who saw her as a confidante. I don't think mum quite understood me, although she loved me dearly. I was more like my dad and she'd never understood him either.

In many two-sister families, 'teams' or 'sides' develop, with mum on one side with one sister, dad on the opposing team with the other. Often this is treated lightheartedly — I remember in my own family we always found ourselves on the same sides when taking family 'bets' on the Oxford and Cambridge Boat Race. But it *can* be another way of competing for parental love, and the depth of conflict and jealousy at such a young age can be staggering. Both sisters need to feel they are someone's favourite.

Jackie Onassis was very much her father's favourite: she was older and more mature, and said to be more like her warm-hearted father; whereas younger sister Lee, said to be more practical and down-to-earth, teamed up with 'her coolly methodical, less emotional mother'.

Hannah Smith was six, and younger sister Katie just three, when their parents split up. But for Hannah it meant she could have mum all to herself again:

> When our parents divorced I went to live with mum and Katie stayed with dad. I only saw Katie occasionally, but I didn't mind as I had mum all to myself, like I had for three-and-a-half years before Katie came along.

Betty, 56, comments on her childhood with older sister, Margaret:

> I always felt my sister was close to my mum; they were so compatible and I thought perhaps Margaret was her favourite, but then I knew I was the baby and so extra special to her. I don't know quite how it would have been if there had been a third sister.

Sue Anderson knows the answer to that:

> My eldest sister got all the attention first, then I arrived and everyone made a fuss of me, and then Carol, so I wasn't the baby any more. I don't know if I was jealous at that age, but I know I didn't like it!

RUNNING TO STAND STILL

A child psychologist once described sisters as a species who are competing with each other like mad for everything they care about. They watch each other's every move in case one is being favoured and indulged, and the most bitter jealousies tend to be between the first two children in a family: the first who must be supplanted, the second who must fight to catch up.

Even a small age difference between sisters doesn't always guarantee a closer relationship. In some families it serves only to increase jealousies and hostilities. In *Hons and Rebels*, Jessica Mitford's autobiography, she brings to life her sisters and refers to their difference in age:

> 'Boud [her name for Unity], Debo and I were too uncomfortably close in age for friendship. We got dreadfully in each other's way in the fierce and competitive struggle to grow up. Boud, three years older than I, hated being classified with me and Debo as 'the little ones'. I in turn tearfully resented being lumped with Debo, two years my junior, as "the babies".'

It was Diana, the third eldest Mitford girl, who was Jessica's favourite sister. She put this down to the fact that there was seven years between them, so they missed each other in the school room and she adds: 'Diana had the necessary qualities for a favourite sister. She was bored and rebellious, all right, a follower in Nancy's footsteps', but she was the one 'inclined to take an interest in me'. She patiently tried to teach Jessica to ride, helped her with piano practice and encouraged her to take up French.

Unlike Jessica Mitford, some women wish they had sisters close in age, so they could share more together. Dawn Wilson, 23, has two older sisters — Pam 31 and Shirley 37:

> It was certainly nice being the youngest, and my sisters did look after me. They tried to protect me as much as possible like when my mum and dad split up. I was only 10, and all I knew was that dad's clothes were suddenly not there any more. They tried to explain it to me as they were obviously more aware of what was going on. Shirley has always encouraged me too, but more in the way a mother might — she'll also correct me and tell me off if I do things wrong. What I really longed for was a sister of my own age, like friends had, so we could make mistakes and share experiences together.

Most sisters seem to feel that a small age-difference meant they had more in common and felt more able to 'share':

> There is a year and eight months between my sister and me. I'm the youngest but I never felt that I was tagging along with her friends — we all seemed to be friends together. I suppose it was because of the closeness in our ages. When I was small I always wanted to do the same things as my sister and to be included in everything. Whenever she announced she was going to do something or go somewhere, I'd say 'and me'. This became something of a family saying and one uncle came to call me 'Little Ann-me'.
>
> *Maureen*

38

Copying an older sister is common (though sometimes annoying for the eldest!). Some younger sisters recall how they used to copy even naughty behaviour, not out of admiration but because they wanted attention too: it didn't seem to matter that the attention would be a good telling off! Wendy still laughs today when she remembers the time her older sister decided to do an impersonation of Al Jolson:

Our dad always preferred us to play in the back yard than on the streets. He could keep his eye on us that way. But there was never much room because all the coal used to be kept out back. Lizzie decided it would be great fun to dress up as Al Jolson, and she covered her face and hands with coal dust. Mum and dad were furious at first, and threw her in the tub, but dad roared with laughter afterwards. It seemed a great way to get attention, so when the next load of coal was delivered I did an action replay. As you can imagine it didn't go down too well at all!

SOMEONE TO LOOK UP TO?

An older sister is seen as a role model from a very young age. Take Amelia, the 8-year-old sister of Sarah Brightman. Still at junior school, Amelia can't help but look up with admiration to her superstar sister Sarah — 18 years her senior — who has enthralled audiences with her performances in *Phantom of the Opera*. You can imagine she'll soon be staging her own mini 'operas' at home.

You can't ever imagine Princess Diana wanting to emulate anyone else's behaviour, but as the youngest of three sisters it appears she saw Jane (four years her senior) and Sarah (six years older) as role models. Born in July 1961, Diana was just six when her parents' marriage broke up and she must have looked to her older sisters for support and protection. She was still at school when the eldest, Sarah, was hitting the headlines for spending a skiing holiday in Switzerland with the Prince of Wales and the Duke of Gloucester.

The newspapers were intrigued: who was that 'tall, beautiful, willowy girl' who accompanied Prince Charles to polo matches and Sandringham? Diana loved it so much she started a cuttings book of her sister's gossip column stories! The press were to find much more to write about a few years later when it was not Sarah, but younger sister Diana who was seen at the side of Prince Charles.

So, it is not uncommon that younger sisters often feel proud of elder siblings. One sister remarks: 'I didn't want to do the same things she did: just being *her* sister was quite enough for me.'

The Spencer sisters with the headmistress of their school. (Courtesy Press Association).

Another woman remembers the pleasure she derived from an older sister:

> I was always proud of her: 'That's my older sister you know', that sort of thing. Our closeness came from the way we were brought up. Mum and dad never tried to make us compete against each other or compare us. We always got the same and always felt equally loved, so there was never any jealousy.

The older sister is often the more domineering — according to the younger anyway:

> Joan was the bossy boots! She was always the leader, and I enjoyed bathing in her reflected glory. I would love it when someone would ask if she were my sister. Although we looked alike and were often taken for twins, I used to wonder why I was not more like her. I always felt she was brilliant.
>
> *Sylvia*

SOMEONE TO LOOK DOWN ON!

Author Deborah Moggach believes the power of superiority an older sister possesses is immense:

> It's a bit like reaching the sixth form, and looking down at the new arrivals in the first year. After years of looking up to my older sister, suddenly Bryony was born. She is 11 years younger, and it was a great relief to have someone looking up to me. I felt I'd reached the sixth form!

Another famous writer, Simone de Beauvoir, expresses the power she felt over her younger sister. In *Memoirs of a Dutiful Daughter* she describes their relationship, saying that she found most pleasure in the 'real hold over her'. 'She only endowed me with authority; adults sometimes gave in to me; she obeyed me'. When they played games, her younger sister was her accomplice: 'A partner was absolutely essential to me if I was to bring my imaginary stories to life . . . I imposed them on my sister, assigning her the minor roles which she accepted with complete docility'.

Likewise Peggy, the eldest of the three Kelly sisters, was always the leader. In Gwen Robyns' book on the life of Princess Grace we learn that when Peggy rewrote Cinderella, *her* script had the main characters as the ugly sisters played by her and her friend. Middle sister Grace was handed the part of Cinderella, who Peggy had ensured 'had nothing to do except sit and look sad'.

Mel Appleby, of Mel and Kim fame, says she had to put up with older sister Kim telling her what to do. She nicknamed her the 'schiz' because:

> . . . she's a real Jekyll and Hyde. One minute she'll be happy, then she loses her temper with me. She's still a bit of a bossy boots. I used to hate it when she ordered me about. I just wanted to get bigger so I could get her back!

As far as Kim was concerned, Mel should have been grateful:

> It was more a question of me trying to give her the benefit of my experience!

POOR BABY

So should we pity the younger sister? Is she the one who suffers a childhood of being bossed around, of imitating the elder, of continual resentment? Well, that's only half the story . . . It's quite common for younger sisters to be treated more leniently, spoilt and indulged. Studies have shown that parents are often more easy going, flexible and relaxed with younger sisters than with the first-born.

Top model Twiggy was the baby of her family. There were three girls born at seven-year intervals, and Twiggy, as the youngest, says her father used to really spoil her, and not surprisingly she loved being the baby of the family.

Bonnie Langford is another 'baby':

There are 10 years between the eldest, Cherida, and me, and 18 months between Pet and Cherida. When I was a baby I kind of had three 'mothers' to look after me — my mother and my sisters! I'm told that when I was a baby I never cried. I'm sure it was because I knew there was always someone there, so I felt very secure.

Jean, the second eldest of four sisters, says Marie, the youngest, was given a much easier childhood:

There was quite strict discipline in the house when Colleen, Teresa and I were all growing up. We had all left home and got married when Marie was just 10 or 11, so in a way she had a totally different upbringing to us. She had a lot more of her own way. For instance, even my younger brother wasn't allowed to have a motorbike when he was in his teens, but Marie got one. I don't know that my parents spoil her more or gave in intentionally, but they were older then and probably just too exhausted after bringing us up!

Pat recalls how in her teens she always had to be in by a certain time, but for younger sister Sue it was different:

I suppose because Sue was growing up in the sixties and attitudes had changed from my teens, she had a lot more freedom. I think she was a more positive person than me, too, and would say 'I shall be late tonight,' whereas I accepted my father's orders.

Agatha Christie was described as the much-loved afterthought when she was born in September 1890. Her sister Madge, older by some 11 years, was sent to boarding school near Brighton and left Agatha as the focus of their parents' attention. She would write letters home to Agatha, who she affectionately called 'my dear little chicken': 'Who do you get to make you a big bath of bricks in the schoolroom now that your two devoted slaves [Madge and brother Monty] have left for school to learn their lessons?'

Sadly she did miss out on the companionship often found between sisters closer in age, yet she still loved her sister dearly, and was slightly in awe of the wonderful jokes, pranks and disguises with which Madge would liven up the school holidays.

Likewise Antonia Fraser, eldest of the daughters of Lord and Lady Longford, was seen by her younger sisters as a distant storybook character and they lived somewhat in awe of her. There were eight years between Antonia and the next sister, Judith, who shared her bedroom with Rachel (Billington) and Catherine, the youngest. The threesome never had time to themselves as they had no space of their own, whereas older sister Antonia lived quite separately in a flat below the Longford family home.

It has often been reported that Princess Margaret was given more freedom and was more indulged in her antics, as the younger of the two. Elizabeth was the King's pride, his heir, and she spent more time with her father, developing her sense of duty and devotion. Margaret spent more time developing her extrovert personality, and was not reproved for being less conscientious or dutiful. Their governess appears to have found Margaret more difficult to discipline, and sometimes her pranks and outrageous behaviour caused her big sister great embarrassment. Margaret simply delighted showing off even more!

Some say she was indulged to compensate for being the youngest, which may also have been the case with Princess Stephanie of Monaco. Royal observers noted that Princess Grace lavished more of her time on Stephanie, their third and youngest child. She always wanted to ensure that Stephanie had as much as big sister Caroline, and that they were treated fairly as they grew up in the idyllic pink walled palace of Monaco. When Stephanie became interested in gymnastics, she arranged for her to be taught by a professional. 'Caroline had her ballet classes and now Stephanie has this'. said Princess Grace at the time.

As the younger sister to Caroline there must have seemed little left for Stephanie to do. As a result she often appeared shy and sulky — observers called her wayward — and she was expelled from finishing school. But it was still jet-setting Caroline who took the headlines. Stephanie was reported to be wildly jealous of anyone claiming her mother's attention, and her death in the tragic car crash in 1982 must have left Stephanie distraught. She had always been something of a rebel against her role as princess ('My mother gave up stardom to become a princess, I want to do the reverse' is a much quoted remark) but her mother's death caused her to grow up fast.

Now it was Stephanie who started to make the headlines, while Caroline stepped into her mother's role, as so many older sisters have done before her. Confronted with crisis, she has become the strong one of the family, and everyone has noted her increasing sense of duty and commitment. Some say her change of lifestyle is uncanny — the way she holds a bouquet of flowers, or shakes hands at royal receptions is so like that of her regal mother.

Despite Stephanie's many varied talents, her attempts at asserting her individuality will probably always be seen in comparison to her big sister. Even so, many younger sisters believe it's best being last in line. Older sisters are great for getting you out of trouble and explaining things:

> I was too soft when I was a child and my older sister would always defend me. I relied on her to get me out of trouble. She always explained things to me too. If there was something I wanted to know I would ask my mum, but my sister always explained things better!
>
> *Sylvia*

Indeed, royal commentators have said that it was Princess Elizabeth, older by almost five years, who explained to Margaret the abdication of their uncle, the fact that their father was to become King, and that, as the eldest, she was in line to become Queen. Hard for the country to comprehend, let alone a six-year-old girl. But clearly she grasped all she felt was significant and was said to have told a friend: 'I used to be Margaret of York, and now I am nothing'. Her sister, always superior by age alone, had now taken another step up.

But as the eldest Elizabeth was also protective of her little sister, anxious to include her in everything. Sir James Barrie, the famed author of *Peter Pan* was known to have remarked on Princess Elizabeth's pride in Margaret whenever she won a game. In Celia Clear's *Royal Children from 1840-1980* he was quoted as saying: 'It was like the pride of a mother though it began, to my eyes, when both were little more than babes.'

Other younger sisters talk about how they have benefited from the protection of a big sister:

> Sue and I have always been close. She is four years older than me and always used to look after me. I remember she went after someone who had beaten me up, and she would always stick up for me which was nice. But her and Mo, my oldest sister, didn't like it if I tagged along and wanted to play with them in the street — they'd tell me to go indoors. As three sisters we all used to argue like mad over really trivial things: once mum walked out in despair and we were all hanging out of the bedroom window crying and screaming! Twenty minutes later she was back: she'd just walked round the block to calm down, and the next day we were all at it again!
>
> *Carol*

I'm glad I was the younger sister because I found I learnt from the older ones and their mistakes. I saw things when I went out with them, and thought 'I'm not going to do that'. I think it makes you grow up more quickly and in some ways I feel I'm more sensible than they are. I sometimes feel like I'm the older sister.

Penny

It's been great being the youngest. I never get blamed if anything goes wrong in the house and I've really been spoilt. But there are drawbacks. Now, whenever I go out I get lots of hassle: where am I going, who with and what time will I be in? I wouldn't mind if it was just my parents, but my two older sisters do it too.

Catherine

With three older sisters, I think I found friends of my own age too childish. I made friends of their friends, and was into clothes and make-up and boys much earlier than most of my friends.

Jane

Other sisters have said they, too, found themselves growing up quickly to catch up with older sisters, often in an attempt to be considered 'old' enough to be included in their games.

SHE'S BEEN LIKE A LITTLE MOTHER TO THEM

It's more usually the older sister who is expected to be responsible, to 'mother' the younger ones, and in some instances take over the 'maternal' role — particularly in families where the mother has to work, leaves home or dies while the children are still young. It can involve immense responsibility at a young age.

When Deborah, the youngest of the Mitford girls, was born in 1920, Nancy — the eldest daughter, then 16 — was made her godmother. This was not unusual in large families; in the event of the mother dying the eldest sister would then step in.

Other women remember:

When my mother died I was 14. My eldest sister was 17 and there were much younger brothers; and she took over the housekeeping duties. Even now she finds it difficult to think of herself — she is always worrying about us.

Liz

45

As the oldest sister with three younger sisters and two younger brothers, I was expected to be very grown up and responsible from the time I was about 11. While my friends were becoming experts with skipping ropes and roller skates, I was a dab hand with the iron. I was expected to look after my three younger sisters, as mum had a young baby to look after. I was mum's little helper. I had to grow up very quickly and I came to resent it as I missed out on so much of my childhood. I was 29 before they reached an age when they didn't need me any more. Strangely I was not delighted, just devastated.

Alice

The tragic story of Catherine Dunbar, who died from anorexia nervosa at the age of 22, was told by her mother, Maureen, in the book *Catherine*, and in Thames Television's dramatization. It was Catherine as the eldest sister who took on the running of the household when their mother left home, convinced she was doing the best thing for her family. Catherine's father recalls how she took over the role of wife, and also mother to younger sister Anna. She would cook the family meals, but would eat hardly anything herself.

Anne Scott remembers the days when she prepared meals and took care of her younger sisters:

During the war my mum had to work nights. I was in service at the time and the family I worked for were moving to Anglesey, but my mum wouldn't let me go. I had to stay home and look after the family. Although I probably missed out on a lot of things, I remember I quite enjoyed it at the time.

One younger sister remembers the pressures on the eldest:

My mother was ill around the time she was expecting the youngest and my father was self-employed so he couldn't afford to be at home. Colleen got landed with a lot of responsibility for us. It was an awful lot for a 16-year-old to take on.

Large families are now not as common as they once were. Before the First World War it was usual to find families with four or five sisters; now it is more common to find pairs. Emotionally there is said to be great strength in being a member of a large family: a crisis seems so much smaller when it can be met by everyone, and there's always someone to rely on. There may also be less jealousy and rivalry too: even if you fall out with two of your sisters, you could be sure there was always one more you could pair up with.

Floss, 84, remembers her sisters:

> We had such a happy childhood in the Kent countryside. I was the middle sister of three and we lived in a country inn with a lovely orchard surrounding it. We used to have to walk a long way to school through country lanes and played happy games on the way. I was the favourite of my father. He used to call me his little Flora-Dora. I was the first one to resemble my father's side of the family. There were eight of us in all, and I don't remember any jealousy between us. My mother devoted all her time to caring for us and we were a very happy family.

Anne Scott says she and her family did everything together:

> My father was a miner and when the pit closed we would have to move on somewhere else, so it seemed best to make friends of your sisters as they moved with you. I always assumed people got on with their sisters. I had Mary who was three years older, and two younger ones, Lily and Margaret. We would go to school together and wait for one another after classes. We used to plan what to do in our school holidays — Mary and I loved walking and often we would go to Sherwood Forest. I was 11 when Mary went into service and I did miss her. When it was her afternoon off I used to go and stand by the gate of the house where she worked until she came out. Then we would walk home and all have tea together.

SISTERS ARE FRIENDS AS WELL

In large families spaced over years, there are often two 'generations' of sisters. Win Mitchell of London, now in her fifties, looks back to her happy childhood with three older sisters. The closest in age was 10 years older than her:

> Although we were a happy family always, I never found close companions in my sisters. They were too much older, and I suppose I looked up to them as somewhat remote.

Peggy was one of a 'second generation' in a family of seven sisters. But instead of great closeness, she strived to do something different:

> I didn't want to be told 'You're you like your sister.' I didn't want to be another clone. So I tended to be a bit of a loner.

Jessica Mitford had strong views, being the second youngest of six: 'Of course, I longed to be a lone orphan' and she felt that having lots of sisters was a 'great toughening and weathering process — it prepared one for later life'. Her eldest sister Nancy once said how she pitied small families: 'When I hear of the Pill, families of two and so on, I feel so sorry for future generations — nobody to stand between them and life's cruel circumstances'.

Within large families, there is often no need for external friends, sisters providing all the companionship necessary — a self contained unit. At Swinbrook House, the Mitford sisters found it 'neither necessary or, generally, possible to leave the premises for any of the normal human pursuits'. They learnt together and played together. 'Seven of us children (including only brother Tom) for mutual human companionship.'

Among the three youngest (Unity, Deborah and Jessica) it was considered that the company of one another was 'amply sufficient'. 'Except for rare visits from cousins, the three of us were brought up in complete isolation from our contemporaries', writes Jessica in *Hons and Rebels*. 'Unity, Debo and I were thrown much on our own resources. As a lost tribe, separated from its fellow men, gradually develops distinctive characteristics of language, behaviour, outlook, so we developed idiosyncracies that would no doubt have made us seem a little eccentric to other children of our age'.

Here there is a likeness to the Brontës who, in their isolation, must have seemed somewhat strange and nervous to outsiders.

Jessica and Deborah Mitford started their own exclusive 'club', the Society of Hons (Hons derived not from honourables, but from the hens their mother kept to raise money for their education!). With Unity, Jessica had a secret language — Boudledidge (after Boud, Jessica's pet name for Unity). A secret language or code words is quite common between sisters, and the Mitford girls found it was a great escape when talking to each other in front of adults!

A present day example of sisterly closeness, to the point of exclusion, can be found in top British group Five Star, which comprises Doris, Lorraine and Deniece (three sisters with one year between them) and younger brothers Stedman and Delroy.

Five Star could well have been 'Thrée Star' as the girls were originally going to form a group on their own much like the Three Degrees. As Five Star their success has been phenomenal, yet it was only in 1987 that they moved away from their overcrowded family semi in Romford. But they stayed together, moving to a £1,500,000 mansion in Berkshire where, for the first time, the girls each have their own bedrooms. Deniece says: 'We wanted a place where we could all still live together but each have a bedroom.'

Even now they share everything (including the occasional midnight feast in Doris' bed) and do everything together: buying clothes and make-up, going to the theatre, watching TV. Some have said their world is too introvert and private, and criticize their closeness but they reply: 'The problem is a lot of families are not as genuine as they used to be.'

Their closeness is incredible in any circumstances, and more so bearing in mind their success. The girls have often said how they are a complete self-contained unit with no time for friends outside the family.

Says Lorraine:

> We've always cared for each other — the bigger the family the stronger the bond. If there's just two of you, you go off with your own friends and never see each other. But with a big family you don't need friends.

Doris, the eldest, adds:

> Some of the children at school couldn't understand why we were always together. If there's one child in the family, then you go out and make friends, but it's like we've got our school friends at home. We all get on with each other and you don't need anyone else. A lot of girls used to be jealous that we three got on so well. We'd play in the garden together and think up strange games that only *we* could play.

In families where sisters play together constantly, a much closer and warm relationship is seen to exist in later years. Psychologists believe younger sisters can gain a great deal from being included in older siblings' games, which are often great imaginary, fantasy adventures:

> My sister Joan was two years older than me and she was very inventive. She would think up lovely games to play. We would play 'Mrs Joan's and 'Mrs Sylvia's' and another game where we were two fictional ladies called Greta and Primrose. Now I realize the games we played were progressive, and provided me with great scope. My mother would let us play with everything: we used to get out the step ladder, turning it into a 'house'; and we would play 'mermaids', making underwater caves with bedsheets and pillows. Sometimes she would go out of the room having left me tied up to a bed post, and forget all about me! But that was okay by me. I would have been very 'alone' without her as she gave me so much pleasure as a child. I never minded her taking the lead and quite liked the fact that I trailed around after her. We each had a doll but only one pram and she would always push the pram but let me hold the handle and I thought that was marvellous! My father

The Queen and Princess Margaret. (Courtesy Camera Press).

used to come along and say 'That's enough of that, let Sylvia have a turn,' but I never enjoyed it as much when I was pushing it!

Sylvia

We used to pretend we were the royal sisters, Elizabeth and Margaret, and our younger brother was our butler. It was great fun. We used to dress up in some of mum's old clothes and hats, and sit in the garden while he brought us lemonade and cakes. We would talk about the weather, Buckingham Palace, the Crown jewels, and who we were going to marry!

Mary

A WORLD OF THEIR OWN

While these sisters were pretending to have royal blood, the real little princesses were enjoying fantasy games of their own. Their father, George V, was always keen that his daughters would have as much fun as other children, and they particularly relished playing 'hide and seek'.

Their antics were supervised by Scottish nanny, Marion Crawford, whose memoirs *The Little Princesses* have long provided an insight into the world of Elizabeth and Margaret as children.

It was fortunate they found so much pleasure in each other's company: their position made it difficult to make many friends outside the family, and some observers have commented on the isolation of their childhood. Christopher Warwick spent many hours with the younger sister for his book called, quite simply, *Princess Margaret* and he wrote that their childhood seemed full of happy memories, love, friendship, and like most sisters, a degree of rivalry. Both girls loved dressing up for charades and the famous pantomimes at Windsor. Margaret was perhaps most inventive in their games, creating a character called 'cousin Halifax', who she would blame if ever she were late, or missed lessons!

They played great games together with their favourite collection of toy horses: 'Pretending to be horses was also a favourite game and . . . the princesses would take it in turn to put on a jangling harness and pull one another around the garden paths.'

But like most sisters, they fought too:

> Deliberate provocation, like Princess Margaret plucking the elastic of her sister's hat (or vice versa) was sure to guarantee battle stations. At such times Princess Elizabeth would pinch and Princess Margaret as the smaller, would retaliate with a kick. 'I never won,' she remembers.

The Brontës must rate among the most famous of all sisters and their well-read words have secured them an honoured place in any book written on the subject of sisters. It was a gift to their brother Bramwell that first started them on their writings: a box of 12 wooden soldiers which their father brought back from Leeds. The sisters had always looked to each other for happiness, because they had no younger relatives or friends. But for each other, they would have had a very lonely childhood. They had no playmates, but they wished for none, and the childish games they played together became, according to Dr Phyllis Bentley who has studied their lives, 'a dominating fantasy'. And so they lived in two worlds: the reality of their secluded life at Haworth parsonage, and their life of adventure and endless talk of wars and battles in the mythical islands of Angria and Gondal.

The stories were written into miniature books (more than a hundred still exist and you can see some of them at the museum within the Haworth parsonage in Yorkshire). Some of the books were only an inch and a half long — yet some pages were crammed with up to 1500 words! They hand printed their words onto tiny folded sheets of paper which they stitched to make tiny books, backed with paper of sugar-bags or shop wrapping.

This was just the beginning for the three sisters, Charlotte, Emily and Anne, who went on to write *Jane Eyre, Wuthering Heights* and *Agnes Grey*.

There were in fact five sisters: Maria, the eldest, and Elizabeth both died (aged just 11 and 10) from tuberculosis and it was Charlotte who, at 9, found she had to take on the responsibility for her two younger sisters, Emily Jane who was 7, and Anne, 5. Yet Charlotte was said to have enjoyed managing the home, and had great ambitions for herself and her sisters.

Some sisters have taken the fantasy games and private worlds to bizarre extremes. Most notably Jennifer and June Gibbons, known as the 'Silent Twins', who wrote countless stories, diaries, novels, drawings and poems, and spoke only to each other, in the small bedroom they shared. One journalist referred to the Gibbons girls as the 'Black Brontës', for they also wrote detailed adventures and plays for their dolls, in a world only they could inhabit. One Christmas they even made miniature books which they filled with Victorian verse and mounted in pretty Christmas tags.

Marjorie Wallace, whose life has become entwined with the twins since she first wrote a newspaper article on them, has read all their diaries — sometimes 2,000 words were crammed on to an exercise book page in minute writing similar to the Brontës.

In her book *The Silent Twins* Marjorie records how, at 16, they spent all their time playing with dolls, and arranging parties and 'outings' for them. Eventually they would speak to no-one but their dolls, and to each other.

The sisterly bond, when taken to this extreme, can be destructive and damaging. But, whether rivals or allies, no-one can describe sisterhood as dull.

Chapter 3

I'm Not a Bit Like Her!

<u>HOW DO SISTERS EXPRESS THEIR INDEPENDENCE? HOW DO THEY</u>
<u>FEEL ABOUT BEING CONSTANTLY COMPARED WITH EACH OTHER?</u>

BEING YOURSELF

One 10-year-old said of her older sister: 'I don't want anything to change, I don't want to grow up, I want things to stay as they are'. Perhaps she had an insight into the years ahead and the inevitable conflicts and loyalties. It's one thing fighting over your Sindy doll, its another when it's your first boyfriend. As you get older you can look back and laugh at how you pushed each other aside to be the first one to get into the Wendy House. Rather more is at stake when the Wendy House is replaced by university.

When sisters reach their teens, some of the accepted practices and loyalties of childhood are replaced by the desire to be 'individual'.

> When we were younger we got on reasonably well, I think you just accept each other more, but as we get older she irritates me more and more. I'm very straight and say exactly what I think and that seems to cause friction, but I just find her very false.
>
> *Susan*

Michelle remembers how she was quite content to let her older sister run things when they were younger. But by the time both girls were in their twenties Michelle was starting to make a stand: 'I wasn't going to be bossed about any more. I think it came as a bit of a shock when I didn't give way.'

Similarly, Joely Richardson, the younger of Vanessa Redgrave's two daughters, appeared to be the quieter, shyer one who had tended to get elbowed out of the way. Until, that is, she started showing she could be as strong-willed as her older sister, Natasha.

YOU'RE VERY ALIKE, YOU KNOW

Often sisters strive to be different and, when asked if they are like their sisters, will adamantly reply: 'no' — and genuinely believe it. With the years come increased differences:

> As we were growing up we started to realize how different we each were. People think we're alike as we have certain things in common — we all have similar laughs and voices, and all have a hilarious sense of humour from our father. And we're all very optimistic. We go blotchy when we get nervous, we talk fast and nasally, and have big eyebrows. But we all look different: I'm small, wear boyish clothes, and feel frumpy next to my younger sister Julie, who's tall, blonde and glammy, and smells of perfume — like something out of Dallas. When she walks into a restaurant, the manager will be there within five minutes asking her out. I'm there for an hour and I'm still waiting for a table!
>
> *Lucinda*

> Wendy and I both went in to nursing and worked at the same hospital — but never at the same time. Wendy had left by the time I joined, and another nurse said she couldn't believe how much alike I was to a girl she used to work with. It turned out to be Wendy. We didn't think we looked alike, but apparently we have exactly the same mannerisms. We talk just the same: on the phone people always mix us up.
>
> *Gillian*

> There's only 13 months between us, and we're both Virgo, so we're bound to be quite alike, but it's as though she's got certain qualities and I've got the others! I'm Virgo in the sense that I like things to be perfect. I'll get an idea about something that I'm really mad about then it wears off. Whereas Marianna is a lot more easy going; but once she's decided she wants something she'll go after it until she gets it. She's got great tenacity. She's also got a winning way with people and is at ease talking to strangers. She comes across

as very open and warm, whereas I'm more reticent, and some times come across as stand-offish, when I don't mean to be.

Jessica

If we fall out, which isn't often, I will rant and rave and get it all out in the open, whereas Anne will stonewall you, which I find really frustrating — it's probably the only thing that really annoys me about her.

June

I brood about things whereas Katie is different — she is like mum who will blow her top and then, in five minutes, it is as though nothing has happened. I wish I were like Katie in that she doesn't get so stressed up about things. I get so depressed. Katie lets things 'wash' over her. She doesn't take things so seriously.

Hannah

WHEN THE COMPARISONS HURT

It's okay for sisters to look at each other and make comparisons but it becomes more hurtful if it's outsiders or other members of the family who make the observations. As the comparisons are made, so inadequacies are born and jealousy sets in.

Alexandra Connor is a painter and author. Her first novel *The Witch Mark*, told the powerful story of how jealousy almost destroys the lives of two sisters. Here she recalls the early jealousies she felt for her older sister:

It always seemed that when she was at her best, I was at my worst. When she was 17 and I was 14, I thought I was horrendous, while she seemed so beautiful and grown up. I had to wear thick glasses, while her eyesight was perfect. I was the one with braces on my teeth, while hers were perfectly in order. She was slim, I was fat and spotty. Her hair was smooth and glossy, mine just frizzy. I truly believed that beauty was the key to everything and determined how much you were loved. A pretty face was everything — that's why my sister was so popular.

But life changed, and the jealousy subsided, when Alexandra discovered contact lenses:

For the first time I could see my face properly, and it wasn't as bad as I'd always imagined.

Everything started to swing Alexandra's way: she dieted, left home to go to boarding school, and away from the comparisons, her confidence grew.

Marjorie Proops remembers the early jealousy she felt for her *younger* sister, Josephine:

> Now we laugh and talk about it, and I confess to Jo that I was jealous — she always seemed the pretty one, and I plain. For example we both have a pretty broad gap between our front teeth, but hers is beautifully straight and mine is crooked. We both had dark hair, but hers had lots of golden glints and mine was mousey brown. And *I* was the one who had to wear glasses from the age of 9. Everything seemed quite unjust, so we quarrelled and fought a lot.
>
> In order to compensate for what I considered to be my big disadvantage I worked harder at school. I did better. Not that I was any more intelligent, but I spent longer at it. It seemed my sister didn't have to work as hard to be successful. I can still remember my mother introducing us by saying: 'This is Jo, my pretty daughter, and this is Marjorie, my brilliant one'. She only said it once or twice but it stayed with me.

Barbara Woodhouse recounts a similar but, for her, devastating experience when she met her grandmother, who lived in Paris, for the first time. She took one look at the 13-year-old Barbara and exclaimed 'You are hideous'. In her autobiography Barbara says she already knew she was ugly for she once overheard her mother say to the nanny, 'Why can't Barbara be pretty like Dene and Hazel?' Obviously Barbara was not meant to have heard this, but as a result she said she no longer cared how she looked, and turned her attention to animals.

Hannah and her step sister Katie had a similar experience, which appears to have affected Hannah more deeply:

> It was mum who was responsible for a lot of comparison. She would say 'Kate is my beauty and Hannah is my brains' which really got to me. I always felt unattractive and thought my hair was dull and mousey and my face spotty, whereas Katie never had a blemish, and mum would look at her and say 'my lovely Katie'. It has taken me a long time to accept that I am attractive in my own right, but I'm still very sensitive to other people's reactions to the way I look, and I don't think I'll ever get over it.

Katie, too, was affected:

> For a long time I felt I was the stupid one. People always expected me to get lots of 'O' levels like Hannah, and I felt great pressure from my family to do better academically.

GOING TO SCHOOL

It is school that suddenly provides a world outside the home. Now children are much more used to pre-school playgroups, but in the past, the classroom was really the first place sisters would come into daily contact with other children outside the family.

At school it is often when differences really start to emerge and most comparisons are made.

> Joan was clever but she was very naughty at school. I was the more academic one, but although I think the teachers found her a handful, I think they admired her for not being cowed down if she was not the guilty one, whereas I was the sort of person who would do anything for a quiet life. I won a scholarship at 11 and she won a place at technical college a year or so later. We used to win prizes; one of us would win one year and then the other the next, so there was never any great rivalry.
>
> *Sylvia*

Sometimes parents compensate for one daughter's lack of academic skill by trying to encourage and help her to do as well as her sister.

> I could never understand why, when things were difficult for my younger sister, Marianna, at school, she'd get more attention. I was trying to play it by the book and do well, and it was very much 'Jessica can cope', so no-one paid any great attention to me. I remember it was the end of my world if I got one sum wrong, but it didn't seem to get me any attention!
>
> *Jessica*

Hannah recalls how younger sister Katie was the naughty one, and seemed to get away with so much more:

> Katie was so crafty — she was really naughty at middle school, but because she looked like an angel, with masses of curly blonde hair like a little cherub, she got away with it. I suppose I was quite moody at school and I was the one who got into trouble with the teachers. I'd look at her and know that she'd got away with far more — but everyone thought butter wouldn't melt in her mouth!

Dawn's sisters had left home by the time she started secondary school but:

> Mum still used to compare us. I've never been 100 per cent at schoolwork. So she used to get out Shirley's schoolbooks and try

57

to get me up to her standards. I didn't really mind at the time, as Shirley is 13 years older than me, and had already left home. I think it would have been much tougher if she'd only been a year or so older. As well as mum helping me along I've had Shirley too. She was the one who got me an interview for my first job. But she can be a bit short tempered with me sometimes, if she thinks I'm doing something wrong.

The expectations that you will follow in the path of your older, 'bright spark' sister can be daunting, particularly when you start at the same school:

I always felt a bit resentful because Sue was the brainy one — the smart Alec who could do no wrong. I suppose I was the dunce, and although mum and dad didn't make me feel that, it was hard when I went on to the same school as her. She was four years older than me, and people would say 'You're Sue Anderson's sister' and because she was in the netball team, and played rounders, tennis and javelin they added, 'so we expect lots from you!' In some ways I felt proud but at the same time a bit resentful. Mum and dad didn't put pressure on me, but in an affectionate way I was the clown of the family — I made everyone laugh. That's stuck with me — I have a cavalier attitude and people think I'm good for a laugh. But I often think even now I wish I was as bright as Sue. My husband Dave thinks I'm a bit of a dunce, and doesn't give me an awful lot of credit either.

Carol

Lucinda Siegar remembers how marvellous it was suddenly to have her younger sister join her at boarding school:

I went to boarding school when I was 10 and I was one of the youngest there. I think one of my older sisters, Louise, was a bit jealous of me as she didn't go to boarding school, but the age difference was too great for there to be be any real competitiveness. I didn't miss my sisters really as I loved adventures. I used to read Enid Blyton and so I was intrigued by the idea of boarding schools — I remember the *Fifth Form at Malory Towers*, that kind of thing. I was 16 when my younger sister Julie started at the same school and I can remember I was so excited to suddenly have her with me at school. I was really protective of her. It was also the year that our father died and it was a very hard time, but it helped having each other.

IT'S NOT FAIR, YOU ALWAYS GET BETTER MARKS THAN ME!

If you're at the same school, you always end up bringing school reports home on the same day. One sister remembers:

> Our father used to sit at the tea table and read them out loud, one at a time. I used to squirm with embarrassment — not because mine was bad but because Valerie's was always much worse than mine. I hated being the goody goody.

Comparisons of schoolwork seem to increase as the age difference between sisters decreases: hence for twins it's almost unavoidable. Research has shown that sometimes differing abilities in sisters, and twins in particular, can stretch the less academic one to reach her sister's standard — but it can pull the cleverest sibling down to the level of her less clever sister.

One mother of twin girls insisted her daughters were put into separate classes at secondary school. One of the twins remembers:

> Throughout primary school I was always thought of as much quicker than my sister Taiwo, and on her reports it would say Taiwo has made 'good progress but not so much as her sister'. I never felt any competitiveness but then I was always in the first division and Taiwo in the third. Our mother insisted we were in separate classes when we went to grammar school. I can still remember that first day; we were in the assembly hall and they read our names for each class, and Taiwo's was in a different one to me. I could feel tears in my eyes — for a few minutes anyway.

SISTER OF THE BETTER KNOWN . . .

Once out of the classroom, it's hardly surprising that some sisters deliberately avoid following in their sibling's footsteps. They don't want to be seen to imitate, and want to avoid the inevitable comparisons and rivalry. But they also have the desire to be seen as an individual, not just as someone's sister:

> We both wanted to join the forces but I knew we'd end up being compared and competing for the rest of our lives. So I took a secretarial course instead, and while my sister is based in Hong Kong, I'm typing memos for my boss in Peckham!
>
> *Hilary*

But it's not always so deliberate — sisters *are* individuals, and they have individual ambitions.

Take Anna, and Karen who is three years younger:

> I've always been ambitious and wanted to get on. Karen and I both want to do completely different things. We are just so different and I think we get on so well because we're not after the same things. I certainly couldn't stand that as I'm too competitive!
>
> *Anna*

> I definitely want to get married and have children, whereas Anna is career-minded. She sees about one man a year she likes and I see a dozen I like. I will still have a career, but it's secondary; with Anna her career is 'first' and marriage is pushed somewhere into the future.
>
> *Karen*

Inevitably, as one sister goes on to achieve great things, others can feel left behind, left out of the action. In 1983 a psychologist invited the wrath of younger sisters everywhere when he announced that first-born children are more likely to succeed. Certainly the press have a field day routing out the younger or older sister who lives in the shadow of their famous sibling. More often than not, the unknown sister will shy away from talking publicly about the one in the spotlight — and who can blame them when, either way, they are made to appear to resent their sister's success? If they share a surname, they're assumed to be cashing in on the other's success; if they change their name and claim their interests and ambitions lie in another direction, they're accused of being rebellious and resentful. Joan Fontaine, the younger sister of Olivia de Havilland, had little choice in the matter of her name. When Joan was also offered a contract by Warner Brothers, both her mother and Olivia said she must turn it down. In her autobiography, aptly titled *No Bed of Roses*, she writes:

> At home, mother agreed with Olivia that I simply could not accept this opportunity. Warner's was Olivia's studio, her domain . . . What's more I must change my name — 'de Havilland' was Olivia's, she was the first-born, and I was not to disgrace *her* name'.

Growing up amid a famous sister's much-publicised activities can't be easy. The pressures of fame can often change family life. Louisa Croft is the younger sister of tennis star Annabel Croft. Annabel sometimes spends just two months a year at home in Farnborough, Kent. The rest of the time she is away from home training, or playing in international matches. Louisa says she remembers being picked up from school and having to go straight to Annabel's matches in the evening. Her mother's

Joan and Jackie Collins. (Courtesy Keystone Collection).

dedication to Annabel's career meant the younger sister had quite a few babysitters. She laughs now when she remembers how her school couldn't believe it when she was the only girl who turned down the option of a visit to Beckenham tennis club.

Singer Lulu had also admitted that her success had definitely affected her family's lives, but whether for better or for worse she couldn't say.

SHE'S MY SISTER, YOU KNOW

For the famous sister it's tough too. If she says she doesn't want to talk about her sister, it's assumed there must be bad feelings between them. In truth, she might just be extending her privilege to a bit privacy. Some people who have read Joan Collins' autobiography have concluded she must be jealous of sister Jackie, who is only referred to in a few fleeting passages. Her very absence causes curiosity.

In fact it was *Jackie* Collins who, in 1960 when still trying to become an actress, declared she had changed her name and was sick and tired of being 'Joan Collins' sister'. But when she stopped acting and started on her writing career the 'little sister' label went away, and in its place 'success'.

The odds against two English sisters becoming so successful in America must be, in Joan's reckoning 'billions to one'. They now both have individual success and between them they share a pact that they will not comment about each other. That didn't stop the newspapers reporting on a 'sisterly feud', which the sisters denied as 'absolutely ridiculous', over Joan's literary plans to get her own book published on life among big time Hollywood TV types. Best selling author Jackie has no real cause for concern: her own book *Hollywood Wives* was one of the fastest movers of all time.

In Anita Dobson's (Angie Watts in TV's *EastEnders*) book *My East End*, she refers regularly to her parents whom she turns to in moments of crisis and who now live near her in Wapping, but there is little mention of Gillian, her younger sister by nine years. She refers to how EastEnders used to have big families with eight or ten children, but Anita's post-war generation saw noticeably smaller families. But the East End has been described as one big family. When Gillian was still tiny she went missing, and Anita remembers how 'every inhabitant of the flats turned out in a mass search for her — until she was eventually found "visiting" a neighbour.' Gillian's name for Anita was 'Panda Eyes' as she wore make-up like Dusty Springfield, concealing all her facial features and lips. There were just two black eyes, hence the nickname!

When an older sister has been incredibly successful, people can't wait for the debut of the younger one. Samantha Fox has said of younger sister Vanessa, 'No-one in the world has got such a fab little sister as I have'. If the tabloids had their way we'd all know just how fabulous she is, as she'd have appeared splashed across their centre spreads. Their father, Patrick, who has master-minded much of Samantha's success, wisely says he's keeping the wraps on Vanessa — she's only 15 after all.

Selina Scott has always kept her private life just that: private. Few people know anything of her family as her younger sisters have not been forced into the public eye. One of them, Fiona, says she is often approached to talk about her famous sister but prefers not to. However a mention in the newspaper diary pages proves that Selina has always encouraged Fiona who, while big sister was presenting the popular fashion programme *The Clothes Show* in 1987, had opened a small studio in Helmsley, Yorkshire, for Fiona is interested in painting, and supportive Selina has bought some of her still lifes for her London flat.

Sandra Chalmers says it's never worried her that her sister Judith has the public face:

I've always admired her and been so proud of her success. It makes *me* feel special when people ask if I'm any relation.

She says it usually happens when she hands over her charge card in Marks and Spencer!

Mijanou Bardot, the pretty younger sister of Brigitte, once said: 'For me she was always famous. She was always winning games, making scenes, so I thought it was natural that she should be a star. I was proud to see her name and admired her'.

Elizabeth Jackson is very proud of her older sister Glenda — so much so that she doesn't always tell people: 'I think it sounds as though I'm bragging.' Naturally Elizabeth has seen all her sister's films. In particular she remembers going to see her first one, *Women in Love*. 'I was so nervous for her when I went in that I thought I'd have to leave.'

CAN'T YOU DO SOMETHING ELSE?

When sisters choose to follow the same profession, or one wants to emulate the success of the other, problems begin and there's bound to be rivalry. Natasha and Joely Richardson are the daughters of Vanessa Redgrave and film director Tony Richardson. Both are talented actresses, but it was Natasha who first determined to follow in her mother's footsteps, while Joely, the younger by 18 months, was interested in sport. Anyone in Natasha's shoes might have felt a stab of jealousy when Joely decided to go in for the same profession. Natasha has described it as 'a slight ruffling of the feathers' which passed when she realized Joely was serious. Both have since had success: Natasha in Ken Russell's *Gothic* and the stage production of *High Society*, and Joely alongside her mother in the film *Wetherby*.

Sharing the same ambitions has brought the sisters closer. Each goes to watch the other's previews — and you can't a get more honest critic than your sister. They both wonder what will happen if they ever go for the same parts, as happened with mother Vanessa and sister Lynne. They competed for Oscars too, but didn't fall out. Hopefully Joely and Natasha's relationship will be a repeat performance.

Julie Kate Olivier is probably *her* older sister's sharpest critic. When she saw Tamsin Olivier in one of her first plays she went backstage and told her 'Well, at least you weren't embarrassing.'

Both girls are daughters of Sir Laurence Olivier and Joan Plowright. They both opted for their parents' profession despite some attempts at dissuasion. Tamsin recalls that, as children, it was to their advantage that their parents were preoccupied with their careers. 'because they didn't rely on us or try to live their lives through us. We grew up feeling freer — and ended up choosing the thing they least wanted us to do.'

NOBODY KNOWS YOU BETTER

Actress Dervla Kirwan is one of the bright new stars of the screen. She was born in Dublin and, at 16, has already won roles on film and stage. She takes notice of her critics: her two older sisters, Paula and Blanaid.

> When my sisters criticize me, I'll crib about it, give out about it — that's slang for moaning — but I'll accept it because nobody knows you better than your family.
>
> Blanaid came to see me on stage in London in *Handful of Stars*, and she said she enjoyed it — and not just because I was in it. She's honest. I value her criticism so I always listen carefully to what she has to say.

Both her sisters still live in Dublin and she says:

> I do miss them now I'm in London. When I'm away from home I keep my feelings inside but at home I can voice my emotions. My sisters sometimes have to tell me to turn down my voice. I'm closest to Paula — she's seven or eight years older than me. I think there tends to be a stronger bond between the eldest child and the youngest. We used to side against poor Blanaid when we were younger.

Dervla sees her sisters as friends:

> Great friends. There's something more, something special. The keenest memories are of family crises — when someone dies or someone's ill — and good news, for example, when Paula passed her exams or Blanaid passed her driving test. The most important thing is that we converse, we communicate. We talk about difficult things and give each other advice.

Sometimes the sisterly advice helps bring Dervla down to earth.

> I think it's important that people get a good kick now and then to remind them who they are. As an actress you tend to think you could be higher up than others, that you are superhuman. With sisters you can't get a swollen head for long!

Tracy Ward is the younger sister of acclaimed actress Rachel. Both girls were brought up by their nanny at the family home in Oxfordshire, as their parents spent a lot of time in London. Tracy was always the rebellious one, who liked breaking rules, and people said she was a bad influence on Rachel. With her independent character Tracy was adamant that people didn't just think she was following in her sister's footsteps when she decided to take up acting. But the person she was most wor-

The Beverley Sisters (Courtesy Syndication International).

ried about was Rachel — what would *she* think? So she phoned her, and Rachel said, 'Great, you must do it' — and said she'd like it more than anything in the world.

Tracy went on to success on TV's *Cat's Eyes*, starring alongside Leslie Ash, whose sister Debbie is also an actress. Both girls were brought up in Streatham, South London, and went to the Italia Conti Stage School. Although their lives are quite separate, they are good friends, and are always there to support each other. In 1986 Debbie was knocked unconscious in an horrific head-on car smash. Leslie Ash was filming at the time, but the moment she heard the news she rushed to the hospital to be with her.

And so sharing the same profession can be seen to bring sisters closer together rather than driving them apart. Indeed as a united force, sisters can be a formidable team.

The Beverley Sisters credit their mother for their long-term success: she brought her three girls up as a team, instilling in them the real sister spirit. Jealousy, she told them, is one of the greatest wreckers of happiness, and she would say to each of them: 'A little less "I" and a little more "WE" please!'

The three Langford sisters all opted for the same profession: dancing. Cherida has a successful stage career, and Pet runs her own dancing school. But it is Bonnie, the youngest, who has become the 'star'. She says:

> We did at one time think of doing an act together, but we couldn't agree on what we wanted to do, so we didn't get around to it. Although it might seem that I have been the most successful in so far as media recognition is concerned, they have achieved so much that is really important: they both have two lovely daughters. When I got the part in *Cats* it was so exciting, but one of my sisters was having her first baby and that was the important thing for all the family.

Others find they can quite happily work together without feeling the need to compete. Take, for example, Harriet (oldest by three years) and Matilda Thorpe, two young actresses in their late twenties. They have starred together as sisters of a rich Californian family in a unique stage show which was a spoof of the great American soaps:

> We love each other too much to feel threatened by each other's talents. I think we had to make a decision, that we're not going to let sisterly rivalry get in the way, so if we do get the odd twinge of jealousy, we talk about it and laugh it off. We respect each other's talent. You can either be threatened, or forget all about it and think: 'I'm so proud, this is my family!' It really gives you strength when you love and respect each other and want things to go well. We encourage each other and find new talents and confidence within ourselves.

Originally Harriet trained as a ballet dancer whereas Matilda always wanted to act. Even before she went to drama school she showed all the brochures to Harriet:

> I thought she'd be a brilliant actress and I wanted her to do it too. I got her an audition and, in fact, she got a place before me! We've both been successful in our own right: last year she appeared at

the National Theatre and I was in the West End, but the soap opera is the first time we've acted together, and it's brought us together immensely. We're quite different in looks and manner and complement each other very well. If there are any problems we can just talk about them and it's over in two minutes. But sometimes we're meant to be rehearsing and we get very chatty, and two hours go by and we don't feel like working. Our parents find it extraordinary to see their two daughters playing sisters on stage. After this I will miss the ease of working with someone where there are no barriers, or no need to tread carefully.

Clearly competition only thrives when sisters envy each other's success. Camilla and Lucy Wigram would agree with that. They are identical twins who, for a time, lived together in London where they both worked as models — their talents inevitably alike. Camilla is now working for an estate agent, and Lucy still models around the world, signed with a top agency. But, says Camilla, there was never any competition. 'It takes two to compete, and she never would'.

However it is often competition that spurs sisters on to even greater success. Joan Fontaine wrote that both she and her sister Olivia were 'achievers', and that 'our impetus may well be the sibling rivalry . . . so perhaps without it we might never have striven to excel, might have been quite content to be housewives or schoolteachers'.

I DID IT FOR THEM

In her early school days, TV presenter Jayne Irving felt little was expected of her, because of her sisters Helen and Catherine who had Down's syndrome; then it spurred her on to fulfil her parents' expectations:

I felt that nothing would be expected of me at school. I had two Down's syndrome sisters so what could one expect? I always found teachers never expected much of me — I always knew I was not very bright but eventually that feeling made me want to achieve more. That feeling intensified; after a while it became a spur to achieve things and fulfil my parents' expectations. I think I felt this much more powerfully than an only child who normally has to carry these expectations, because of my parents' disappointment. But they never pushed me to do anything at all.

My parents felt there was something wrong with them having two Down's syndrome children. Being Catholic you feel you have done something wrong: that it's a sign from God that you have sinned. They were just delighted when everything was all right with me. I still feel the need to achieve and make them proud of me.

My mother had always told me my sisters were handicapped and that they did not behave like other children of their age would do. I think when you're a child what you want more than anything else is to conform, to be like everyone else. When I was much younger it was quite a shameful thing: it was really something I was embarrassed about, particularly when I was only 5 or 6, when I began to realize that my sisters were not like others. I do remember I got quite spoilt at Christmas when we had lots of toys as Cathy and Helen were not interested — all they wanted to do was eat!

My older sister Helen, who could walk, was quite rowdy, disruptive and she was always trying to run away. In fact my mother said that it was me who'd taught Helen to walk! But she did not realize the dangers of roads and we had to keep an eye on her.

Eventually it became too much for her parents to cope with: Jayne's mother was also looking after her elderly father, so when she was eight, they both went into homes. Jayne says the attitude to mental health was different then, and has only changed in recent years:

It was felt that if you had someone mentally retarded then you put them into an institution, and that has resulted in generations of parents who have felt very guilty. At the time my parents were told it was the best thing to do and that places didn't come up very often. In different times they might have stayed at home.

Cathy went to a place in Sheffield and Helen to Derby. It was very odd not to have them around anymore. I did not really understand what was going on even though my parents tried to explain it all to me. They wanted me to have as normal a life as possible and said that it was up to me if I wanted to visit my sisters, which I did.

After a while it just became the norm that my sisters did not live at home. I had the experience of being an only child, and there was none of the usual rivalry between siblings. It was a long time before I could talk about it with friends. I would never mention it openly but now I can quite easily, but sometimes other people are upset by it. Perhaps at a party someone will ask if I have brothers or sisters and when I say, 'Yes, they are mentally handicapped', I sense their embarrassment, so sometimes I don't mention it.

I also found that I formed incredibly close friendships with other girl friends at school, and then later at university and at work. I think I was doing this as some kind of compensation for the special relationship with my sisters that, in a sense, I had lost.

SOMEONE TO TURN TO

Sisterly relationships can be strengthened or weakened by family traumas. The effect of crises such as sickness, divorce or death of a parent during childhood or adolescence can have a complex effect, but sharing the pain and confusion does appear to lead to increased closeness among sisters. In particular the divorce of parents, can lead to closeness — or to conflict:

> Rosa and Ellen, who are my two half-sisters by my father, became closer when their parents split up. They are very different personalities, and are now a duo in their own right. They 'feed' off each other's strength. I think that is very important.
>
> *Becky Howard*

> Our dad died when I was 13 and Abby was 16. She lost a lot of weight and I was really worried about it. She's so thin anyway, but she went down to six stone and I made it my responsibility to feed her up. I wouldn't say we actually became closer when dad died, because we were close anyway, but we became more protective of mum, and now we're more like three sisters, and mum comes out with us, and we're rather a lethal trio.
>
> *Jo*

> We'd always tried to get on for the sake of our mum who'd brought us up alone, and we felt it reflected on her as a sense of failure if we didn't hit it off as sisters. But when dad went everything just fell apart. Suddenly we both wanted all mum's love and attention and we bitterly resented each other. When mum died we went our separate ways. We didn't hate each other. We just didn't feel anything.
>
> *Kim*

In crisis the traditional childhood roles come to the fore again. Though the age gap may have become less significant, and sisters have become 'friends' it is still the eldest who takes on the role of protector:

> Not so long ago Jo had a panic attack about work: a very minor type of breakdown I suppose. She just couldn't go into work so I took time off to stay with her: to me it was important because she needed me. Now whenever Jo is going to do something she's going to regret, I try to step in. Like we were out together once and Jo saw her boyfriend out with another girl. Jo was drunk and I had to get her home and lock her in to stop her doing something I knew

she would regret. She wasn't very happy at first, but she thanked me the next day!

Abby

I'm so protective it drives me nuts — it is probably because mum left home a couple of years ago and I feel more responsible for Katie. If she is going out with a boy I sort of vet him and I get worried and feel I have to give her advice. About six months ago these three guys kept ringing up for Katie, and she says I used to get uptight and moody about it. I suppose I am more like that than she is, but I think it's partly being the eldest.

Hannah

Kim Appleby is the eldest in the Mel and Kim duo. When Kim was 15 and Mel just 10, their parents' marriage split up and, with their mother, they took refuge in a hostel in South London. Kim was very much the older sister and went out of her way to get Mel a job when she left school at the same clothing factory where she worked as a machinist:

That probably caused our worst row ever. We were meant to clock on at 8:30, and she used to turn up at any hour — 9:30, 10, even 11 o'clock one day. I felt she was letting me down and I suppose, as the older sister, I felt responsible for her.

Kim adopted the caring role of older sister even more when it was recently discovered that Mel had a very rare form of cancer affecting her spinal cord. Kim was with her all the time, sleeping overnight at the hospital, by her side when she came out of surgery, and when she took her first steps after the operation which could have left her paralysed. Doctors made it clear that Mel would need plenty of love to help pull her through, and it went without saying that Kim became ever more protective of her 'little sister'. In fact, a recent American study found that cancer sufferers are much more likely to survive if they have the support of a loving sister or partner. Mel moved in to her sister's holiday flat during her illness, and Kim has since said that they are now even closer than they were before.

Gillian Taylforth who plays Kathy Beale in TV's *EastEnders* has an amazingly close relationship with her three sisters, but was slightly alarmed when she started playing the protective role with her youngest sister Janice:

Once I started telling her off when she stayed out late. And then I thought, this is crazy — I'm getting worse than my mum and dad!

Mel and Kim, taken when Mel was recovering from a rare cancer. (Courtesy Syndication International).

The youngest sister is often considered the 'baby' all her life. Peggy remembers how she hardly noticed the growing years of her younger sister Grace Kelly. She told Gwen Robyns, the author of her sister's autobiography: 'She never went through a gawky stage. She was not too tall, nice and slim, and no skin problems. She went from Girl Scout to belle of the ball without us noticing it. In her sweet and quiet way she had a million beaux.'

But you can't help but notice your 'little' sister has grown up when she starts wanting to wear your clothes.

FIRST UP, BEST DRESSED

When American writer Elizabeth Fischel asked women, 'What's the angriest you've ever been at your sister?' as part of the research for her book *Sisters*, the answer she got more often than any other was to do with clothes: 'She's always borrowing my clothes', 'She ruined my new dress', 'She stole my favourite shoes'.

Anna knows just how they feel:

> I remember when I was 16 and Karen was 13 she seemed a child and I thought I was grown up, but now Karen wears all my clothes and drives me potty. I have got a job and she hasn't, so I don't mind, but sometimes when I've bought something new I would say, 'Please don't wear that'. I had this new pair of trousers and said don't wear them. What happens when I come home? She is wearing them, and worse still, leaves them in a crumpled heap on the bedroom floor!

Twiggy was much the same. As a teenager it was the middle sister Viv who was the neatest and tidiest. Regardless, Twiggy says she would take her 'newly laundered and pressed sweaters and wear them for the evening and then put them back without telling her'. She even remembers once borrowing a pair of Viv's shoes and lending them to a friend!

Carol was one of four sisters and remembers that, as they got into their teens, clothes were a really bad source of arguments.

> Natalie, the oldest, used to have the most fabulous clothes and all three of us would 'nick' her stuff to wear out. She always used to have the best cosmetics, like Dior, and I used to think I'm going to have some of that. She used to go mad, she's very pedantic anyway and she always noticed if something was not put back right! Now my young sister comes and stays with me and sometimes she borrows my clothes and leaves them on the bed for days and days, and that makes me mad even though I'm not that houseproud.

> I spend a lot of money on clothes and always seem to buy the wrong thing. Abby can buy one thing and it's fantastic, but she lends me anything. Sometimes she'll buy something and I borrow it before she's even worn it, then we forget who it belongs to in the first place!
>
> *Jodi*

Gillian Bullock has two sisters; Wendy is three years older and Catherine four years younger. Gillian says it was only when she moved into a flat with her boyfriend that she first realized how few clothes belonged to her!

All three of us have always shared a bedroom which is horrible *but* nice! I think it makes you closer as sisters, and we'd often lie in bed and chat until the early hours. We've always shared everything and that includes clothes. When I left home and packed up my clothes I found I had to leave two-thirds behind as they belonged to Wendy and Catherine. It was then I realized how few clothes I actually had.

Kim Appleby remembers:

The first thing we rowed about was toys, but most of the time we argued about clothes. When Mel was about 13, she always used to 'nick' my gear 'cos I was out working and buying decent clothes and she was still at school.

CAN I COME?

It comes as a bit of a shock when 'little sis' doesn't only want to wear your clothes, she wants to come out with you too. Your little playmate is replaced by someone to go to clubs with, to do 'keep fit' together, or to go on holiday with. Several sisters have also said that nowadays it makes sense to have someone to travel home with too.

An older sister is a 'ticket' to a grown up world — to clubs and parties they couldn't go to on their own. Mandy Smith, singer and one-time girlfriend of Bill Wyman, was going out with the older sister Nicci to late night clubs by the age of 13. Likewise, Penny, a 20-year-old stylist at London hairdresser Ocean Boulevard, said she was always quite happy to go out with her older sisters:

Mum always encouraged us to go out together when we were younger, which suited me because it meant I could go to clubs and places with my two older sisters who are now 21 and 22, which probably I wouldn't have been allowed into on my own. The other two were always borrowing boyfriends, but I've only borrowed their clothes, and even that causes a bit of friction.

Wendy and I were often taken for friends rather than sisters, and we would go out together. Although I'm three years younger I'm 5' 10'' and have always looked older for my age.

Gillian

73

> In our teens we used to go out on double dates with two fellows who were friends, one of whom was the more dominant who used to go with my sister Joan, and I had the quieter one.
>
> *Sylvia*

> When Carol was 18, she and her friend came on holiday to Greece with me and my friends. It was her first proper holiday abroad without mum and dad, and I think mum was pleased that she was going with 'big' sister, but they were a handful!
>
> *Sue*

Not all sisters take so easily to the idea of having their younger sisters tagging along:

> We never really got on when we were younger. We used to go to school on the bus and I'd totally ignore her. I always thought she was childish and so much younger than me. Now I can see she felt left out — she always wanted to come out with me and our two brothers. It was in the sixties and we used to go to parties. We said she was too young to come and she resented it. Fortunately she didn't wear my clothes: at that time the scruffier you looked the better and I've never been clothes conscious since. My parents clamped down more on her — I think because they saw how I was turning out!
>
> *Jane*

It's not surprising the younger sister likes to be seen with their 'older' relation. As one sister recalls, her elder sister was certainly a person to be seen with:

> She had men, not boys, coming round for her. She used to wear stiletto shoes, have her hair in a 'beehive' and once I even saw her come home on the back of a motorbike!

In her profile of Margaret Thatcher, Patricia Murray shows how even the Prime Minister lived some of her early life through her older sister Muriel. She says: 'Having an elder sister meant that I was introduced to everything before she was'.

Muriel went to Birmingham to study physiotherapy and Margaret, just 13 at the time, missed her greatly. But through her older sister's experience she learnt about a life they had never known. She continues:

> Although she only received minimal pay, she soon discovered how to make the most of it and where to find the best buys in clothes. Muriel soon found her way round the big city shops and my

knowledge of make-up really began when she started to give me the odd glamorous thing for Christmas, such as a powder compact.

YOU DON'T LIKE *HIM*, DO YOU?

It's over 'looks' and 'boyfriends' that sisters seem to enjoy teasing each other most. Jessica Mitford in *Hons and Rebels* recalls how the eldest, Nancy, was particularly sharp-tongued and sarcastic.

> 'If one had taken particular trouble to do one's hair in ringlets, she was apt to remark: 'You look like the oldest and ugliest of the Brontë sisters today' . . . When we grew up and were coming out, her favourite tease was to find out whoever it was that we fancied — which she always managed to do, whatever our efforts at secrecy — and then tell us that she had seen him at a dance the night before, where he proposed to her.'

Deborah Moggach remembers her eldest sister reproaching her for her taste in men:

> I can remember covering my walls with pictures of Dirk Bogarde, and my eldest sister coming in, giving me a withering look and saying 'You don't like *him*, do you?'

Occasionally the younger sister can get her own back. Dawn Wilson says of her two older sisters:

> I can remember when I was young, I always laughed at my sisters when they brought their boyfriends home. They used to be kissing them goodbye at the front door, and I used to stand on the staircase and make sucking noises. I guess I was lucky — I had no younger sister to tease me.

Annabel and Kim are two sisters very close in age who are determined not to fall out over boyfriends. Kim says:

> We've always had the same friends and the same boyfriends too, sometimes! It had caused slight friction in the past but only very briefly. I don't think we'd like it if we'd had a serious relationship going but it's never been like that. We go out a lot together and we're very in tune, we have the same wicked sense of humour and can be quite outrageous when we're out on the town.
>
> It sounds awful but sometimes when I'm out with my boyfriend I'm thinking that I could be having a drink with Annabel and being more wild. There are times I'd far rather be out on the town with my sister than with a man. I think men are often more jealous of our close relationship, but I don't take any notice.

Annabel adds:

> When she's out with her boyfriend, she's very different, more quiet.
> She sits quietly and behaves herself! Yet I know when she's had
> too much to drink she's terrible, and can get quite bolshy. Men
> usually fancy her first. I end up being a best friend and she gets
> all the action! Sometimes I say to mum, 'How does Kim do it?' I'm
> not jealous, just curious!

BUT HE'S GOING OUT WITH ME!

Stephanie Calman went through similar experiences with her sister
Claire, and you can read all about them in her first book *Gentlemen Prefer
My Sister*. For five months prior to starting work on her book, Stephanie
and Claire went out almost every night, and older sister Stephanie, who
says her sister is twice as attractive as herself, found she was stood up
on more than one occasion — by her sister! She was always getting offers
from attractive young men.

Marjorie Proops says she soon learnt not to bring any boyfriends home:

> They used to be quite keen on me, so I'd take them home to meet
> the family. They only had to set eyes on Josephine and that was
> my lot!

Actress Rachel Ward introduced her younger sister Tracy to the very eligi-
ble Marquess Henry John Fitzroy Somerset — son of the eleventh Duke
of Beaufort, and set to inherit around £100 million worth of land. He
had arrived to take Rachel out for dinner and Tracy was just 15 at the
time. Over 10 years later it was Tracy who took the lead role in what the
Daily Mail described as the 'society wedding of the year': she married
the Marquess on 13 June 1987.

A similar story can be told of the Spencer sisters: for it was the eldest
sister Lady Sarah who first formed a friendship with Prince Charles. Her
younger sister, Diana, evidently had a similar taste in men for it was she
who eventually married him. At the time newspapers reported Sarah
was delighted and declared it a perfect match, 'They will be wonderful
for each other. They will be totally compatible in marriage . . . she will
make a wonderful Princess of Wales'. She also suggested that her youngest sister benefited from the mistakes she made — some say her biggest
was talking to a reporter about her relationship with the Prince.

Lady Sarah was also seen to play cupid for her other sister, Jane. When
her engagement to Robert Fellowes was announced, she was thrilled,
and was reported to have said: 'We had been trying to trap him for years!'

The Spencer sisters did what some sisters would describe as unspeakable: they ignored the unspoken but very present pecking order: eldest sister marries, then so on down to the youngest.

One eldest sister still blushes when she talks about her sister's wedding in 1958:

> I felt as though everyone's eyes were on me, not on Margaret. There I was the poor frumpy sister who was bridesmaid yet again. My sister knew she was upstaging me by beating me to the altar. I never forgave her for it. When I got married I didn't invite her to the wedding and we've barely spoken a word to each other since.

Nowadays, the pecking order can still relate to marriage, but also to the first one to leave home, go to university, pass a driving test and more. It's often as one of these stages is attained that sisters grow apart, the relationship changing as the sisters move forward into their individual lifestyles.

Chapter 4

THE TERRIBLE TWOSOME

<u>ARE TWINS CLOSER THAN SISTERS? DO THEY FEEL TRAPPED BY</u>
<u>THIS? DO ORDINARY SISTERS HAVE THIS BOND?</u>

The subject of sisters has long had pulling power: their differences and similarities, their rivalries, their jealousies. Sisterly love and devotion can make the headlines just as often as sisterly rifts.

Twin sisters make the most headlines, and they've made the record books too! One of the most recent additions to the *Guinness Book of Records* was of May and Marjorie Chevasse who made history as Britain's oldest surviving twins. They made the 100 years mark in August 1986, defying odds of 50 million to one. Born when Queen Victoria was on the throne, they have lived under the reign of seven monarchs! Daughters of a former Bishop of Liverpool, they led quite separate lives, although neither married. Marjorie worked for Dr Barnardo's for 33 years and May, the younger by 20 minutes, became a nurse with the Forces during both world wars. In newspaper reports at the time, they put their secret of longevity down to keeping an interest in life and staying as active a possible.

One of the happiest 'sister' stories in the *Guinness Book of Records* is just two lines long. These lines list the names Hannah, Lucy, Jenny, Sarah, Kate and Ruth. Remember them? The Walton sisters, born at Liverpool Maternity Hospital on 18 November 1983, made history as Britain's first surviving sextuplets. From that day on it was six of everything, but the parents, Janet and Graham Walton, have always been determined that they don't grow up as 'just one of the Waltons', but that each sister develops her individuality. Of course there are lots of common physical characteristics but, by all accounts, personality-wise they're very individual.

The media love sister stories like the Waltons and there's no shortage of them: sisters at double weddings; twin sisters marrying twin brothers; sisters achieving the same school grades; sisters giving birth on the same day; sisters passing their driving test together! There's good mileage in sisterhood — the national newspapers of recent years have delighted in:

- The driving examiner who had the strangest feeling of *deja vu* as Lorraine Baker arrived to take the test. He had passed her identical twin Sharon that morning. 'The examiner told me he had already tested me that morning. I had to tell him it was my sister,' said Lorraine, who then emulated sister Sharon by passing the test.

- Carol Killian and Gail McClure, two Arizona sisters, made the headlines twice—two years running they both gave birth on the *same* day!

- Identical twins Karen and Sandra Keeling married on the same day and then flew off on honeymoon to the same hotel in Malta. Another pair of identical twins, Doreen and Dorothy Addison, went even further. They married twins Colin and Derek Rossborough on the same day in August 1986. They went on honeymoon together and once back home moved into flats next door to each other!

- Jenny Perkins, Linda Morton and Susan Keverne were all christened and then married at the same country church, so they agreed that they should have their babies christened there as well, travelling from London and Hertfordshire to gather at Babworth in Nottinghamshire for the ceremony.

- Jenny and Jacqui Halliday each got 11 passes in the same 'O' level subjects. The girls, who always revised together said, 'We think in very similar ways, so it's not surprising that we got the same results.'

- When inseparable triplets Andrea, Lesley and Jackie Griffiths married in a triple ceremony, Andrea, the eldest of the 22-year-olds by twenty minutes, said, 'Tonight will be the first time we girls haven't all slept together!' But they added: 'The wedding is the last thing we do as a team.'

- An amazing feud between two sisters, sent their brother running for cover. They came to blows over borrowing each other's clothes, what TV programmes to watch and a whole lot more. 'Ever since my daughters could talk they've argued,' said Mum. The local council intervened and bent planning rules to let their brother move in to a mobile home!

SEEING DOUBLE

Of all sisters it is twins that attract most media attention. Twin sisters are one of life's most amazing double acts and rather than feeling incredibly self-conscious about being a 'twin', many actually revel in the attention. In America they've their own magazine called, of course, *Twins*, and hold a lively festival each summer in the Ohio town of Twinsburg.

Until the turn of the century, this town was actually known as plain old Millsville, but its name was changed at the request of twin brothers who donated land to the town in 1817. You could be forgiven for seeing double at the annual Twinsburg get-together, which attracts well over a thousand pairs from around the world. There are competitions (with prizes for the most and least alike, oldest and furthest travelled and so on).

Spotted at a recent Twinsburg gathering, for instance, were one effusive and inseparable pair of 11-year-old twin sisters, Karah and Sarah Isom, complete with twin Cabbage Patch Kids, twin German Shepherds and the same best friend. When Sarah had to go to a maths lesson, Karah begged to be allowed to join her—and they missed the same 8 out of 200 questions on the final exam. Karah once broke her leg and Sarah asked for and got bandages and crutches from the hospital, too. 'We want to get twin houses, twin cars,' said Sarah. 'We want to have the same gardens and live next door to each other.'

Identical twins Karen Braaten and Laura Terheggen think twinship is wonderful too, yet they dislike the inevitable comparisons. At one time Karen even contemplated having her nose changed. When she heard about it, says Laura, 'I rushed to the mirror to say "What for?" '

Sidney Sheldon looks at how comparisons by outsiders can turn twin love to loathing. In his novel *Master of the Game*, he describes firstborn Eve as the 'leader', always the first to do everything, and adopted by her identical twin Alexandra, who copies everything she does. But Eve's hatred for her younger sister takes over; a hatred of looking like her, sharing a birthday with her, dressing like her, sharing in her grandmother's love; and she tries to kill Alexandra the day before their fifth birthday. . .

The fascination of identical twins continues in Judith Michael's book *Deceptions*, which was made into a TV mini-series. Identical twins Sabrina and Stephanie are treated from birth as separate individuals by their mother, who insists that they should not be treated as 'peas in a pod' simply because they are identical. So their rooms are decorated differently, they wear different clothes, receive different presents, and the girls are different. Sabrina is the more adventurous, Stephanie the more cautious. They continue to lead quite separate lives, Sabrina in England, Stephanie in America, until, that is, they decide to swop identities and try out each other's lives . . .

PULLING HER THROUGH

One of the most powerful stories of sisterly love is that of Jackie Fitzgerald and Margaret Wilmore. When Jackie was 23 she was involved in an horrific road crash, and it was her eldest sister Margaret who pulled her through. Jackie had been a passenger in a van which was a virtual write-off after careering off the road and crashing into a wall. The accident in 1984 left her with a broken neck, leg and arm and, on a life-support machine, she was left to battle for her life. Margaret was at the hospital bedside as her sister lay in a coma. She still remembers people telling her that her youngest sister had just a one per cent chance of recovery. But when sisters pull together, the power can be quite intense:

Our mother had died just a few months before Jackie's accident, and none of us had really had time to grieve. As a sister I felt it was down to me. I'd always fed her and taken her out when she was a baby, you see, as I was 12 when she was born. I've always adored and loved her dearly. It's a bond which only sisters can understand. At the hospital I knew she could hear me talking to her, but other people said she wasn't aware I was there. I was sure it was just that she couldn't respond to me.

Margaret had always been a forceful personality but no-one had counted on the strength she showed at that time. 'I literally took over the hospital,' she says now. She refused to allow the life-support machine to be switched off. The many agonizing months of uncertainty paid off when Jackie was eventually allowed home, still with severe disabilities but, with her sister's love, determined to pull through.

She moved in with Margaret and her husband and was still partially paralysed down one side of her body and found it difficult to talk. Margaret could scarcely conceal her pleasure when, a year later, Jackie was able to take steps unaided. But she says, as Jackie becomes more mentally alert too, she gets more frustrated at her limitations. There have still been times says Margaret, when it's been touch and go:

Once she was seriously ill with pneumonia, and we willed her through. If she hadn't wanted to live she'd never have left the hospital. I told her 'If you die, I'll kill you!'

Margaret will often sit on Jackie's bed and talk:

One day I said to her, 'As far as having children goes, I reckon you're my lot, you're my baby.' Jackie said, 'I'm not your baby,' but to me she always will be, regardless of what's happened. I've always thought of her as the baby of the family, and it will probably stay that way.

Like Margaret, sisters can play a more significant role than any other blood relation to their sibling's health. At the age of two, Kristy Green became the youngest leukaemia patient ever to receive a bone marrow transplant, and it was all down to her big sister Adele, who was also one of the youngest ever donors.

When leukaemia was confirmed, Kristy's parents were warned that she could be dead in six months. The only chance was a bone marrow transplant and that meant finding a donor with matching tissue. The chances of finding it were greatly increased because Kristy had three older sisters, and there is a one in four chance of finding the same tissue in each parent or sibling. Adele—Kristy's oldest sister, then aged seven—had the matching tissue and was told how she would be giving her sister a chance to live.

FINDING EACH OTHER

Among the most incredible and heartwarming stories are sisters who have been parted for years, and who are eventually reunited. There was the story of two women who saw each other regularly when taking their young children to school, or at the local bingo hall. One of them found out that her grandparent had adopted a sister who she'd never heard about. She followed the trail from there and it ended at her friend's front door!

Then there were the two sisters, separated 26 years ago, who worked as nurses at the same hospital for five years without knowing the truth. They were only reintroduced when their older brother turned up for treatment.

Many sisters have been reunited with the help of John Stroud, whose painstaking work has brought together 30 pairs of twins separated at birth. It was the Children's Act of 1975 that first gave adopted children the right to know who their parents were. At that time John was a social worker, counselling adopted children who were searching for their parents, and he also came across women desperate to trace the 'twin' sister with whom they'd lost touch. The reunion, says John, is heartwarming, emotional and sometimes a bit of a shock: 'Looking at your mirror image is unnerving,' says John, who often keeps in touch with the twin sisters he's helped reunite.

Barbara Herbert was 33 when she called on John to help her find her sister. John set to work, and eventually a meeting was arranged at King's Cross Railway Station. When Barbara first saw Daphne Goodship she knew it must be her—they were wearing exactly the same outfit. Then they both held up their hands to compare their crooked little fingers! The similarities continued from the fact they both have weak ankles from falling downstairs when they were 15, to their strange liking for cold black coffee.

There are uncanny similarities in another set of reunited twins, Shirley Johnson and Janet James. They were separated at six months, and didn't meet again till they were 43 but both are short-sighted and wear the same unusual style of glasses; they married within two weeks of each other, and have been single parents for the same number of years. Even more uncanny, Shirley had once felt sure her long lost sister had some connection with Warwick Castle, so went there for a day trip. She didn't find her, but when they eventually met up, it was revealed she lived opposite a pub called the Warwick Castle!

John Stroud was also involved in the reunion of Lilian Wales and Betty Leach which was filmed for a TV documentary series. It was their brother who discovered a faded snapshot of himself and two little girls, and that started him off on his search. Separated at the age of two, and reunited in their sixties Lilian said:

> I just knew something was missing. I look back at the times I didn't have Betty, when I had this empty feeling I couldn't define. When we came together it was as though we'd known each other a very long time.

John Stroud, looking back at his work, says he often wonders how many women go through life never knowing they have a twin sister.

Singer Sinitta didn't discover she had a twin sister until she was 21. They were separated soon after birth when their parents split up, and Sinitta came to Britain with her mother. Unbeknown to Sinitta she had been introduced to twin Greta when she was about five:

> My mother used to be in the touring company of a show called *Hair*. There were lot of teenagers in the show and we all toured together. Every kid I met was introduced as 'my sister' or 'my

brother' and there was that kind of tribe-like feel to it, so when we were touring Australia and I met her and I was told 'she's your sister' I just thought 'great, I've got someone else to play with now.' I liked her but I didn't actually think she was *really* my sister.

Fifteen years later, in 1985, her mother told Sinitta her twin was coming to stay.

'What do you mean my twin sister's coming over here?' 'You remember—I introduced you. I told you she was your sister.'

The next thing I knew Greta arrived from America where she's at university. She's known about me all her life, and had newspaper clippings sent to her and everything. For me it was out of the blue but for her it was the moment she'd been waiting for, grabbing me in her arms and everything and I was a bit overwhelmed. I felt really cautious and I think I probably seemed really cool at first.

She'd call me 'sis' and it just didn't feel right—it was all going too fast. She'd come and sit on my bed and start chatting about really intimate stuff and I'd just clam up because I thought 'I can't just share my secrets with you. I don't know you.' She was like a complete stranger—with my face—telling me very personal things. She wanted to be in and out of my closet, sharing everything with me like a sister, and she'd come into the bathroom when I was on the loo and things like that. She felt like she'd known me all her life, and I wasn't ready for that at all.

She came to the theatre and she'd be sitting in my space, putting on my make-up and trying on my wig and costumes. I felt I couldn't say how I felt. I had to be quiet about it which made it worse because if we'd been real sisters then I could say 'Get out of the bathroom' or 'Put my make-up down' and you can scream and shout like sisters do. But 'cos I didn't know her I was polite.

She came over for two months, at a time when everything was going really well for me. *Macho* was No. 2 in the charts, I was still doing *Mutiny*, David Essex and I were engaged, and he would pick me up in helicopters. I'd have limousines that drove me everywhere, I had my own flat and people coming up to me in the street to say hello. She came at a very strange moment because I wasn't used to that either, of course. Then I had a twin sister! I think she got a bit cross sometimes because I think she thought I had the much better end of the deal and I was trying to say: 'No, this has literally just happened, I'm not used to it either.' But she thought I'd always had this very privileged, sheltered and spoilt life. Whereas I'm more experienced in restaurants and clothes and the less important

84

things—show business basically—she was very streetwise. She was a lot bigger than me. She said she really thought I was dinky, which I found a bit irritating! I didn't want to be dinky, especially not to my twin sister.

By the time she left we ended up not liking each other. We were born into the same family but we don't seem to have that closeness and I don't know that we ever will. When she left I started to feel sad and nostalgic. I suddenly thought it's nice to have a sister because it's lonely being in show business and not having a big family. I really want her in my life but don't know how she fits in. If we'd just found out at the same time, we could have got to know each other gradually, and worked at the same pace.

There may be other women, like Sinitta, who reach their twenties unaware of a twin sister. But with identical twins the odds are more in your favour. Nancy Segal of the University of Minnesota explains it can start with mistaken identity: 'Someone says, "Hey I saw you in Cambridge on Saturday", only you weren't in Cambridge on that day.' After a few more instances of mistaken identity, the curiosity sets in.

A SPECIAL RELATIONSHIP

The feeling of most identical twins reunited after years of separation are euphoric about finding their 'other selves'. 'It was like two friends meeting, as though we had always known each other,' one twin said.

Another twin, separated from her sister for 53 years, noted that, 'You wouldn't normally pick up the 'phone and speak to someone you'd never seen before for half an hour, non-stop.' 'We are complete now,' said another.

Some amazing research, begun in America in 1979, looks at this most special breed of sisters, identical twins, in particular those who have been reared apart. Sinitta's experiences would be most welcome and, indeed, John Stroud and the twins he has helped re-unite have helped greatly with the project.

The *Minnesota Study of Twins Reared Apart* looks at the course of a typical 'twin week', plus medical and social life histories (from blood pressure, allergies and eye tests to values and interests). Identical and fraternal twins who were separated early in life and reared apart are invited to Minneapolis. They arrive on Saturday and leave the following Sunday, and during that time it's estimated they answer 15,000 questions!

The result of the full study will not be known yet, but early pilot studies have shown that identical twins reared separately actually become *more*

85

alike than those raised by the same parents together. It's suggested that this could be because they have not had to struggle to be treated as individuals, or lived a life of many comparisons. Instead they have their own friends, activities, clothing and surroundings. Examples so far have included twins with similar voices and mannerisms, like chewing their fingernails; twins who have both liked maths and disliked spelling at school; twins with identical blood pressures, pulse rates and sleep patterns; and twins who share a mistrust of escalators.

In overwhelming numbers, whether they have been reared apart or together, twins are glad to be twins. 'We always warn our friends that they will never be "first". We are, and always will be, each other's best friend,' says Lora Stewart and Linda Longerbone, reared-together identical twins, now co-presidents of the Minnesota Twins Cities Twin Club.

Twins have been described as 'walking laboratories' because they hold so many fascinating potentials for researchers. Identical twins are produced not from separate eggs, but by a single fertilized egg splitting into two, into clones, shortly after conception; so all the genes are the same. Fraternal (non-identical) twins are just siblings who happen to be born at the same time, as they are two separate eggs released by the ovary and each fertilized by a separate sperm. They share half their genes in common, no more than ordinary sisters born of the same parents at different times.

Height and physical traits are more affected by genes than personality and behaviour, although you can't always tell just by looking if twins are fraternal or identical. Blood tests are most accurate, while hand and footprint tests are usually quite reliable.

Researchers can pick and choose as there are probably 50 million around the world! The frequency of identical twins is the same worldwide: one in every 250 to 350 births, whereas the frequency of fraternal twins varies sharply. In the United States they occur once in every 89 white births, but once in every 70 black births. In Japan twins arrive only once in every 200 births; in West Africa, though, twins occur once in every 30 births! In Britain it's once in 100.

Twins are usually keen to take part in research; some have said that in most instances they take well to being the centre of attention and parents in particular are enthusiastic about twin research in the hope it will provide them with some of the answers to the special problems of rearing twins.

It was similar aspirations that inspired Dr Elizabeth Bryan to co-found the Twins Clinic. It studies aspects of bringing up twins and it aims to increase public awareness of the problems peculiar to twins. Since 1976, clubs have been set up throughout the country and from these the organization was established.

The clubs are for parents of multiple birth siblings as well as twins, and it is among those that there has been most increase. Dr Bryan explains: 'There are more triplets and upwards because of these fertility drugs,' but now that the chances of having multiple births is on the increase—although still rare—the first ever national survey into the subject is now under way.

The results should be interesting, and may well help parents with the difficult task of bringing up twin sisters or triplets! Certainly, says Dr Bryan, it is not an easy task, and both parents and children are forever in the spotlight. The curiosity of other people never stops. One twin says how she started to feel that it was not her as an individual that people were interested in, but just because she was a twin, and so she started to lose confidence in herself. Although there can be security in twinship, it can't be easy to know there is another person who is so much like you. It is twin sisters, too, who have the greatest identity problems (yet they are also the ones who share the closest bond).

They are looked at as one person, one unit, one pair, yet they struggle to be seen as distinct individuals.

TWINS ARE DIFFERENT

Yet even identical twin sisters can have very different personalities. If there is any difference in size at birth, then the larger one tends to be calmer, the smaller more demanding, lively and tempestuous. Even more significant on the sisters' later lives is the order of birth. Sarah and Carole Hunt are among the country's top female long distance swimmers. Now 24, Sarah remembers:

> As the oldest of the twins by 35 minutes I've tended to take on the protective role. At school people always came to me first to ask me what I thought—they regarded me as the older sister.

The first names Taiwo and Kehinde are a giveaway to whom was the first born in the George family. Kehinde says:

> Our names mean First Born and Second Born. (More literally it's World Seeker and Comes from Behind.) Taiwo is 25 minutes older than me. I suppose she has always been the more dominant one. Our mother says she has always ruled my life, and taken advantage of me. If ever I stand up to Taiwo mother always says, 'three cheers for Kehinde'. She likes to see me standing up for myself.

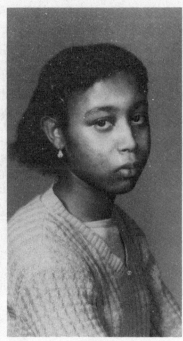

The Gibbons twins, aged 19. (Courtesy Marjorie Wallace).

> But it has never bothered me. Anyway our father was Nigerian and according to an old Nigerian custom, it's the *second* twin who is the senior, not the first. The second twin is the wisest: she pushes the other one out first to see what the world is like!

Marjorie Wallace, author of *The Silent Twins*, suggests the rivalry between the Gibbons twins, June and Jennifer, may have started in their mother's womb 'because there was not room for two of them to grow and flourish there.' The position in which they were born—June head first, Jennifer breech—may have meant that June was literally sat upon by her sister! In their teens a new element in the struggle between them developed.

Marjorie Wallace writes: 'Jennifer was trying to remove any discernible differences so that they would, in effect, become one human being. It was as if she wanted to take June back with her into the womb before their egg had split. She always felt herself to be the inferior twin, 10 minutes younger, less loved by her parents, less favoured by teachers and with fewer recognized talents. As long as June was indistinguishable, the twins were, in effect, equal, and Jennifer felt safe. June . . . longed to be different, to be the prettiest, cleverer twin.'

Staff planned trial separation. 'Jennifer knew this was her last chance to keep June for herself. "You are Jennifer. You are me" she would incant again and again . . . One of the teachers remembers June's terrible cry: "I am June. I am June," as Jennifer forced her to submit.'

June's plea is probably one that is heard in 'twin' households all over the country as twins demand a right to their own identity. Dr Bryan says: 'I know of one father who did not know which twin was which right up to 13 years of age. To me, that is terrible. Even parents, who want their children to be treated as individuals, often forget that other people, say teachers, cannot always identify which twin is which.'

Most experts say that twins should not be dressed alike, and each sister must be treated as unique, with dissimilar names, and never referred to as 'the twins'. They should be encouraged to make separate friends and learn to be independent of one another.

But the pressures can be heavy: one mother of twin girls said she deliberately avoided dressing the sisters alike but everywhere they went people would make remarks, suggesting it was odd not to buy them similar clothes, that she acquiesced. Another mother remembers how she always bought them quite different playthings but the twins would fight so violently to get the other's new toy that the house is now packed high with two of everything!

Twin sisters Valerie and Wendy Holloway say they always dressed alike as children, and they liked it that way. Even now when they go shopping for clothes they buy 'two of everything'. It was Valerie and Wendy who were so alike that they dated the same boy for nine months without him realizing there were two of them.

UP TO NO GOOD

Twin sisters can have great fun: Jayne still laughs at how she and her twin sister used to meet their boyfriends in the same café, and the staff used to stare becuse they thought it was the same girl going out with two different boys in one night! Two identical sisters remembered a friend who decided it would be fun to fix them up with identical twin brothers. 'It was a real freak show,' she remembers. 'People just couldn't stop staring at us!'

Janet and Jackie got up to great pranks in the classroom too:

We were in separate classes, so each week we used to look at each other's timetables and work out which one of us would go to what lesson. I used to hate sport, so Jackie used to take my place—which meant that every Wednesday she spent *all* day in the gym, with her class in the morning and mine in the afternoon. I got far better exam results than she did and no-one could understand why.

Generally people do assume twins have the same academic abilities, but that's not always so, which can cause problems if you are always being compared with your brighter twin sister. All through school you worry about which of you is better: however good or bad the school results are, twins are always compared to each other far more than with other members of the class.

Parents are advised to ask that twins are put into separate classes at school because sometimes the higher ability twin drops down to the level of the lower. Specialists point out that it is important to support the successful twin—the one who passed the exam. Otherwise they can feel terribly guilty about having all the luck.

A fascinating series of experiments conducted in 1934 by Helmut Von Bracken in Germany showed that differences in the amount of work between the identical twins *decreased* when they worked in the same room, as compared with their work output when they were alone. The 'faster' twin would slow down to allow the 'slower' twin to catch up.

This was evidently the case with June and Jennifer Gibbons, whom Marjorie Wallace described as 'like a Rubik cube—when one side does well the other one tends to pull back to her level.'

But this doesn't just happen with academic work: swimmers Sarah and Carole Hunt avoid swimming in the same competitive events because their competitive instincts are dulled by an inherent sense of loyalty. In one race Sarah was swimming much faster than her sister, but dropped back to join Carole in joint third. Says Sarah:

It's certainly true that if we swim in the same race we tend to wait for one another. We both want to win but we want to be equal first!

It's hardly surprising then that twins often end up with identical school results. That's when people start suspecting twins of telepathic thoughts.

Melanie, a twin sister now in her forties, remembers how they were always put into different rooms to do their exams: 'The teacher imagined that we were sending each other the answers telepathically!'

Some twins dispute the idea of telepathic powers. Camilla and Lucy Wigram will tell you about several incidents which others might put down to telepathy, such as the time Lucy had a heart operation as a child, and Camilla experienced pain and fear while her sister was in the operating theatre. But she says it's how anyone would feel if it was someone close: 'You live through it with them.' Other women have experienced labour pains when it's their twin sister who's giving birth.

Sarah Hunt has experienced more than one inexplicable incident: she once gave up her bid to cross the Channel. With almost 25 miles behind her, and only half a mile to go Sarah suddenly lost the incentive to go on. Later she discovered that moments earlier her twin Carole had withdrawn from the attempt with a shoulder injury.

Sarah said:

> We have never really understood it but there have been other examples too, like the time I was taken ill with appendicitis in Yugoslavia and Carole was at home getting ready for the famous swim across Lake Windermere. Suddenly she got these mysterious pains and we found out later that it was at just the same time as I was taken ill. Another time I broke my arm and Carole felt the pain!

Little research has been done on the subject but Dr Elizabeth Bryan says that some of the feelings which occur between twins can occur between husband and wife too.

Marjorie Wallace finds a similar explanation for some of the Gibbons twins amazing behaviour. When they were sent to prison for arson, they were placed in separate cells and could not see each other, yet their movements were 'made in perfect synchrony with the precision of the Changing of the Guard!' Prison officers described their behaviour as spooky, like 'one mind split into two bodies.'

The explanation, says Marjorie, was probably simple: 'The girls spent a lot of time reading and writing and had played their games so long that they would automatically take up "standard" positions.'

The tragic death of two-year-old twins Rebecca and Laura Sankey is harder to explain away. They both suffered from an incurable skin disease, and died within seconds of each other, holding each other's hands. Their parents believe it was a kind of pact between the girls, that they didn't want to live without each other.

American research has described the loss of an identical twin as one of the most tragic and devastating events in the life of the surviving twin. Although neither Rebecca nor Laura could talk, it was as if one sent a message to the other that she was going to die.

TOO CLOSE?

Even when twin sisters do learn to speak, they often need few words between each other, or they develop their own language. Like Grace and Virginia Kennedy who began to talk at 17 months but in a language that was all their own. It's known as Idioglossia, or twin speech, and occurs very occasionally among twins who have had little or no contact with other children.

When Grace and Virginia were taken to the Children's Hospital and Health Centre in San Diego, California it was discovered that the girls had invented their own language using verbs and nouns, pronouns and adjectives!

The unspoken bond, and occasionally a secret language, excludes other people. In fact Elizabeth Bryan says it must be one of the worst fates to be the older sister of twins. The twins' arrival causes so much excitement she is bound to feel left out. The twins are always an 'interest' and a 'pair', while she is set apart.

Sarah and Carole Hunt, have an older sister. Sarah says:

> I think it was difficult for her because Carole and I would always gang up together against her. She was always the one in the wrong, but mum and dad were very aware of what was going on. If people were saying 'what lovely twins' they would always bring her in and involve her as well.

Even parents can feel excluded, according to some twins:

> I think my mother resents the fact that we are twins because we are so close together, and not that close to her. Whereas if we had been born separately we might have allowed her into our relationship as sisters a bit more. I think she really feels she hasn't had a look in.

The closeness between *all* kinds of sisters, not just twins, can be expressed in many ways.

THE GREATEST GIFT OF ALL

Twins will go to great extremes to help each other, and perhaps the greatest act any sister could ever do for a sister has to be giving her a longed-for baby of her own.

The story of a mother giving away new-born twins to her sister Christine Thedoulou made front page news. 'I am extremely lucky to have a loving sister who would do something like this for me,' she said. Her own adopted child had died in a car crash. In a tragic turn of events it was the adopted child who had also been borne for her by one of her other sisters. Christine said at the time: 'It was typical of my sister to help us. It is the finest thing one sister could do for another.'

Anne would have given her oldest daughter to her childless sister, but for her husband:

> My sister went to live in America and my daughter spent six months out there with her while she was still very young. She wanted to keep her, as she could not have any children of her own. Between us we agreed that she could stay provided she always knew I was her mother and that when she reached the age of 14 she could come back to England if she wanted to. I could not have done this for anyone but my sister. But when we started to look into it more closely we discovered that the only way she could take her to the States was by legally adopting her and my husband would not agree to that.

It's an act of love that causes great intrigue—the sisterly relationship, already complex, has to be strong enough to withstand far more tangled emotions. Deborach Moggach studied these feelings in her novel *To Have and To Hold*. It tells the story of Viv who decides she will transform the life of her very ordinary and conventional sister Ann, by having a baby for her. Although Viv appears to be doing something very noble, Deborah says she was also being very manipulative, wanting to place her sister's life in order. She admits that in some ways Viv was an 'unflattering portrait' of herself, because over seven years ago she had offered to have a baby for her childless younger sister, Alex:

> I had two children at the time and that seemed plenty for us, but there was poor Alex desperate to have a child. Without an enormous amount of trouble it seemed I could change everything for her. There was the element of domination, of being able to order your sister's life for her. I suppose I have always been the bossy one but none of my sisters has ever taken orders from me. It was much more than that anyway—it would have been such a wonderful and generous thing to have done for a sister, wouldn't it?

The baby didn't happen, but *To Have and To Hold* did; and its success delighted Deborah, but at the same time caused her some agonized soul searching:

> I've made a lot of money out of it, and sometimes I feel I used her, and it seemed wrong that I could gain out of her misfortune. But Alex is endlessly generous and says she doesn't resent any of it.

In a strange way, says Deborah, making everything so public helped Alex to come to terms with her childlessness. At the time it had all seemed such a simple and rather logical thing to do for a sister who couldn't have children. Now with test tube miracles and advances in science, a sister who says she wants to have a child for her sibling, doesn't have to go through nine months of pregnancy; the one sister's eggs can be fertilized by the sperm of the other sister's husband, and implanted in to the womb. Indeed babies have been born in this way at the Wellington Hospital in London, which houses one of the country's leading test tube baby clinics.

But in May 1987, guidelines by the unofficial watchdog on *in vitro* fertilization, the Voluntary Licensing Authority, recommended that donations by sisters and close relatives should be avoided, stating that it was preferable for all eggs to be donated anonymously.

Dame Mary Donaldson, chairman of the Authority said at the time:

> A sister signing a piece of paper to say she relinquishes all rights to the child solves nothing. There is still the question of personal relationships. I can visualize a situation where a teenager might say: 'You are not my real mother. I want to go and live with my aunt'.

A final ruling has not yet been made but many sisters must be waiting on the outcome. Two sisters had been ready to contact a clinic to consider them, and the initial ruling was a severe blow. Neither of them could understand what could be wrong in what they had intended to do. Indeed they said they felt it was far preferable to *know* that the donated egg came from your sister than from a stranger. Mr Brinsden, the deputy director of the Wellington Hospital's Vitro Fertilization Unit said in May 1987:

> We find patients like having an egg donated by their sister because they feel they know what they are letting themselves in for genetically rather than receiving a tiny piece of tissue from someone unknown. I personally think that if a woman is prepared to give one of her eggs to her sister to enable her to become pregnant, that is a compassionate and caring thing to do.

Many sisters agree. One said she would far rather have an egg donated by her sister because at least she'd know what to expect, and she added that the child would surely be more like any children she might have had if circumstances had allowed: 'We have similar personalities, temperaments, and even looks . . . you couldn't really get any closer to it being her own child.'

Genetically the baby's aunt is its mother, but experts agree that the real mother is the woman who carries the child in her womb.

Researching this book there have been many instances of selfless devotion between sisters, bringing them even closer together, but surely there can be no act of generosity to match this: it can unite sisters for this generation and the next.

Chapter 5

GROWING TOGETHER, GROWING APART

WHAT HAPPENS TO SISTERS AS THEY GO THEIR SEPARATE WAYS?
DO THEY GROW APART, OR DOES THE CLOSENESS REMAIN?

DOING YOUR OWN THING

For years you've shared the same home, the same breakfast table, the same trip to school, the same holidays, but then comes the moment when everything isn't the *same* anymore. A sister takes a holiday with a friend, decides to get a flat of her own, moves off to university or gets married:

> When I went off to university and Marianna was training to be a hairdresser, we each had our own circle of friends and were totally alien in tastes and associations. She used to call me a snob and I used to consider her a bit of a slob! She used to say to me that I was having a really cushioned environment at university. She'd say, 'You don't know everything about life', and I thought I did, but when I came out of college I suddenly experienced a lot of problems. She was probably wiser at a younger age as she'd been confronting these things by experience.
>
> *Jessica*

It is inevitable that as sisters grow up they go their separate ways. Carol talks of her sisters and their vastly different lifestyles:

> There was Natalie. She wanted to get into the music business or be a ballerina but couldn't, then wanted to marry and have

95

children. She's the only one married—with three kids.

Susan went through her hippy university days—we all thought she was a total alien at the time. Now she's a social worker, and I admire her because she's happy with what she's got. I get bored, and envy the way she can relax and enjoy what she has. I have to exhaust myself to relax, until I'm so tired I can't look for other things to do.

Barbara doesn't have a lot of ambition like me. I always used to go off on Cloud 9 and dream of being successful—I knew that's what I wanted. I started my own PR business when I was 23, and making money is an aid to helping my sisters and my parents. Although our lives have gone separate ways I still feel a closeness and commitment to them. They'd probably tell you I'm very materialistic, but I don't think any of them know the real me. I'm like a cracked wall, cover me up with paper and don't let it show. It's not that I'm frightened to show my feelings but I think it might worry them if they think I can't cope.

Gillian Taylforth and her three sisters are all involved in very different lifestyles: Gillian has her success with *EastEnders*, Debbie the eldest is a nursery nurse, younger sister Kim gave up acting to become a policewoman, and the youngest sister Janice is a single mum. Despite the differences her sisters are 'some of my best friends' she says.

Lucinda Siegar looks at the lives of her four sisters:

We all grew up in Glasgow but eventually all five of us have gone separate ways and our everyday lives are very different: Louise is a housewife in Battersea, Hilary is a theatre sister, Libby lives in Edinburgh and preaches about God, Julie works in Scotland as a secretary, and I'm down here in London. I did live with Hilary for a while in London.

I knew I wanted to go to art school and at 17 the only place on the map where I knew someone was London, apart from Glasgow and Edinburgh. Hilary had just got married and I was living in their basement flat and was so scared to go upstairs, except for once when I thought I'd surprise them with a nice meal. What did I do? I put a plastic bowl on top of the oven and melted it, then tried to defrost some lambs' hearts by grilling them. She was furious with me, but with each other we can really shout, then it blows over.

I think my sisters all love me because I look so like mum, I think it comforts them that if they haven't gone home to see mum for a bit and they see me they feel happier. In a way they mother me, but I don't think any of my three sisters really understands what

I'm doing. They know how much I love it and support me and try to help out when I'm broke. One of them paid when I needed glasses as I couldn't afford it—they look after my health, and send me bits of money or a pair of espadrilles! When I go home and I'm with them they all seem so well-dressed and settled; my life is always in some kind of turmoil and I still don't dress like anyone else!

In some families the differences become irreconcilable. The change in lifestyles, changes in personality, and changes in their once close sisterly bond. One says:

Although we'd been close when we were younger and people would mistake us for twins, we found we had nothing to talk about when Susan came back from university. Whereas it had been our world before, she now had a whole new group of friends and ideas, and we've never been able to revive that childhood closeness.

BEING OVERTAKEN

Growing up and growing apart in sisters has been said to go in order: the older sister gets married first and so she has children first, and so on. Everything's been tried and tested by the time it's the youngest sister's turn. The danger strikes when the younger one makes the first 'move':

When I got pregnant before my eldest sister I knew she was really upset. I phoned to tell her and she said 'You beat me to it' and I said jokingly 'I'm fed up waiting for you.' But I think she really was very upset by it. There were no congratulations, and I think she'd considered it a race and that I'd been guilty of foul play because I'd beaten her to it. When I lost the baby, in an awful way, I think she was glad deep down.

When Lana Wood married at 16, she remembers her older sister Natalie had just one concern: 'If you have a baby before I do, I'll just die.'

Sometimes the growing apart can be natural progression for one sister, and a painful one for the other. Lana Wood recalls in *Natalie*, a memoir of her sister, that she sobbed hysterically when Natalie, then 19, married Robert Wagner. ' "Please don't go away from me, please," I pleaded. "I'll always be there for you. Never worry. You will come and stay with us sometimes," Natalie reassured me.'

Another sister recalls the announcement of wedding plans:

I was 18 when my sister announced she was getting married. In our teens we'd always gone out together; in a way I lived my life through her and think I'd have been very miserable as an only child. So I certainly didn't like the idea of her getting married. I thought everything was going to be different and this man would spoil it all, and he used to think we agreed too much about each other's opinions. He is very nice but I suppose I always thought 'I wonder why she wanted to marry *him*'. But then I suppose that's how it should be otherwise sisters would both like the same man!

She was 20 when she married and had her first child when she was 21. She lived upstairs, and in fact when the baby arrived we were inseparable: as she grew, my little niece would follow me around everywhere!

I DIDN'T REALIZE HOW DIFFERENT WE WERE

Seeing your sister in her new environment with husband and baby is sometimes the first time you become aware of the void that has come between you. Julie McLean is three years older than her sister Shirley, who is married with a young baby Eve.

I recently had them to stay with me and I was holding Eve when Shirley walked in. The baby smiled at her and I was aware of this exclusivity—there was something between them, and I was definitely not part of it. I felt a pang, a stab of envy, not for what Shirley has, but for what I felt I had lost. Shirley and I had been close for a long time, but when she married I felt Shirley pulled away from us and I experienced quite a bit of pain. She is very family orientated and happier than ever. It's as though she's found her niche and I've lost part of her.

In a way Julie says Shirley has now stepped in to the role of older sister:

She talks to me sometimes as though I'm the younger sister. I've said to my boyfriend, Alan, that I don't like the tone of voice she sometimes adopts. I know I can be overbearing and I suppose I've talked down to her sometimes. She probably thinks, 'Right, now she'll get one over on me!'.

WE WANT DIFFERENT THINGS

Julie and Shirley both respect each other's lifestyles: while Julie is building her career in London, Shirley's priority is homemaking. Neither envies the other. It can be more difficult when one appears to have found her niche, and the other is still searching. It was Elizabeth, now the Queen, who first settled into family life. Margaret was just 20 by the time her older sister had two children, Charles and Anne. It was at this point, writes Nigel Dempster in *HRH The Princess Margaret*, that Margaret began to feel quite aimless, and their lives went off at a tangent, as the younger sister took to night life, as opposed to family life.

Those other royal sisters, the Princesses Caroline and Stephanie of Monaco have experienced this situation more recently. Yet Princess Stephanie appears not to be craving the same life as her sister, Caroline, who appears to have settled for family life. 'Sometimes I envy my sister, and I wish I was going home to a husband and children,' Stephanie has been heard to say, but the mood soon passes and for now she enjoys her freedom. In 1986 she launched a collection of swimwear designs, and went on to hit the No. 1 slot in France with her record *Irresistible*. Princess Grace reportedly said: 'Stephanie is going to be the most interesting of all our children,' and it looks like she may have been right.

Some sisters continue to live quite separate lives: one opting for a husband and family, the other for freedom and a career:

> My sister settled for all the sensible things—getting married, having children, buying a car. I've never had a husband, let alone anything as long term as a mortgage.
>
> *Jane*

Occasionally sisters say they have deliberately found themselves following different lifestyles: one choosing the career, the other marriage and children. 'That way we stopped competing all our lives,' says Jane. Indeed some sisters appear quite content to live a part of their life through their sister: the one who has the family is more than happy for her sister to come round and play the 'maternal' role at weekends.

In the Collins' household, the mother of Joan and Jackie worried that her older daughter might never settle down and find a man who was right for her as Jackie had seemed to do. In her autobiography Joan writes: 'My sister was pregnant now, and mummy was thrilled, hinting strongly that it was time I took a turn in that direction.'

BEING MARRIED SHOULDN'T CHANGE ANYTHING

Many sisters are adamant that they will never be split by marriage:

> We both want to get married and have children but we don't want it to affect the family, we don't want things to be different between us. Jo would love us to all live together in a big house with our

respective partners, but I suppose it's impossible—I think there
are few men who would put up with that!

Elaine

It's interesting to hear from sisters who have found that marriage and
motherhood haven't driven them apart—indeed it's brought them closer.
Marje Proops can see *why* this happened with her and sister Josephine:

Once we were both married our relationship changed, suddenly
the competition between us disappeared. I think that implies that
sisters of our generation only wanted to get married and did not
have the same career aspirations as girls today. Ever since then we
became closer—it was wartime and both our husbands went away,
mine to the Far East, and hers to Europe. We helped each other
a lot in that time.

Other sisters recall similar experiences:

At first when my sisters got married it seemed as if I'd lost them.
But then when you go into their homes, see them and accept them
in a new environment, get to know their husbands, you realize
that they've changed but you haven't lost them as a sister.

Anne

Deborah Moggach says she is perhaps closest to her sister Sarah and
they always feel at home in each other's houses:

Her house looks like mine, it smells the same. Her children wear
the same secondhand stripey jumpers, and she keeps chickens.
In many ways we've become more alike: we're all ecological and
earthy. None of my sisters wear make-up except me, and I wear
more with each year. I think they find me a bit flippant and
metropolitan.

Regardless of such small and much bigger differences, sisters are always
there for you. One woman says:

When we were younger we used to argue a lot, there were eight
children, three of us girls. But when we were older and married
we became good friends—we didn't see one another often but we
always knew we could count on one another in an emergency.
During the war my oldest sister took our family into her home
although she had four children of her own and space was tight.
She wrote to me as soon as the blitz started and said we must leave
London and stay with her. We both had one daughter each and
swore that we would take care of each other's child if anything happened to either of us.

Candida says it was marriage and motherhood that meant she had something in common for the first time with her older sister Carol:

> In our teens we had absolutely nothing in common, and I can remember when I was 21 thinking Carol was ancient. She was only 24! Soon after I got married I went abroad as my husband got a job in Dubai, and Carol and I actually started writing to each other. Then, when I discovered I was pregnant, I returned home six weeks earlier than Kenny. Carol was pregnant too, and we spent lots of time together going shopping and planning things. Now we've both got two children and obviously we've got more to talk about. Our two eldest girls, Emily and Katy are incredibly close, not as sisters might be perhaps, but there is certainly something special between them. At first I didn't want them to go to the same school, as I thought they'd always be competing against each other. But they're in different classes and now I'm pleased because I know they've always got each other if they fall out with their friends.

Candida admits she can't help but feel slight pangs of envy when her parents pay more attention to her sister's children, and that she was 'quite pleased to have the first boy'—a legacy from her own sisterly rivalries—but it soon passes:

> Now I might envy her her dishwasher or microwave, but it's never anything important.

As well as the sisterly bond, sisters become 'aunts' and that's yet another link. Judith and younger sister Sandra Chalmers have always been the closest of sisters, but as they've got older, married and had children they've become even closer. Says Sandra:

> We're both family people and my children and Judith's are all great friends. We get together regularly for Sunday lunch, and we wouldn't miss a Christmas together.

Another woman adds:

> Once you're married and particularly when you have children I think your sisters play a bigger part. They become aunts too, and they become part of your children's lives as well as your own.

Bonnie Langford's two older sisters both have children and she loves the role of 'auntie'. She says:

> I love making a fuss of my nieces and when I'm away from home I'm always looking for some present I can take back for them.

Eldest sister Cherida describes Bonnie as a great sister and a terrific auntie:

> Bonnie loves coming home and relaxing with all the family. She's born under the sign of Cancer and that's the sign of a home lover. We find her sitting quietly, with my two girls and Pet's two daughters all rushing around—she just loves it. She's so good to them, bringing them toys, even clothes and shoes—not many young girls would bother to buy clothes and shoes for their nieces, would they? My husband (who's also a dancer) absolutely adores her too. He once said he'd marry her tomorrow if anything happened to me!

GETTING YOUR OWN SPACE

Marriage is perhaps one of the roles that allows sisters a much-needed distance. The same could be said of moving into a first flat; going to university, starting a new job. All allow some breathing space away from the ever-present sister, and many have discovered that it was the early intensity of their relationship that caused most rivalries. Given space, they grow to relax away from parental attention and realize how much they mean to each other. Marianna and Jessica grew apart during university years, but now they're both back in London they live together:

> It seemed only natural. I know I'd be lonely if she wasn't there. We still fight, but in any big crisis I know my little sister is there to help.

Joely Richardson says that she and Natasha were 'poles apart, complete opposites' until she went to America. When she came back, both of them saw changes in each other and found it easier to get on. The distance perhaps allowed them to develop, without the fear of stepping on one another's territory, and they found they both wanted the same things out of life. Natasha is now one of the most important people in Joely's life: 'We really need each other now, whereas we didn't when we were children.'

Amy and Grace Li are two top fashion designers who worked apart for two years when Amy, the eldest, was in Paris. Now they're back living *and* working together:

> Chinese families are always very close. Our father worked with his brothers and it was seen as quite a natural progression for us to work together, as we were both working as fashion designers. But when we were at St Martin's college together I was one year behind Amy. We had our separate friends and not many people

knew we were sisters. In fact I spent a whole year trying to find something else to do other than fashion, because I was aware that people automatically assume you are following each other. But in the end there was nothing else I was interested in or any good at.

Now we're working together it's all coming together. We can trust one another completely, you don't have to worry that one would do anything behind the other's back. There are always disagreements when you're running a business, but we come out and say exactly what we feel, and there's always a compromise. You need to be able to be pretty blunt and unless you know someone well you can't be. We know each other even to the point of knowing what the other is thinking—whether we agree or not is another matter!

We have separate strengths I think: Amy is good at organizing, getting people together, and I stop us spending too much!

Amy adds:

When we're choosing fabrics I want to buy everything and Grace puts her foot down sometimes!

WE HAVE A LOT MORE IN COMMON NOW

For some sisters the twenties and thirties are years of growing separately; in families where there is a very large age difference, sisters often grow together when they are older. Katie Boyle, TV personality, journalist and ex-model, is one example. Her half sister is 23 years her junior, and looks upon Katie as a sort of mother/sister/friend:

I didn't see a lot of Margherita when she was growing up, as I had left my native Italy and was already married in England when she was a baby. But when we met up again and she was in her teens, it was quite extraordinary how we slipped into a close 'belonging' relationship. A friendship developed from then on despite the fact that we still live in different countries and our careers are totally different too. No show business for Margherita, she became one of Switzerland's foremost child speech therapists, but now her second marriage has taken her to Germany where she helps her husband to run his fashion house in Bonn. We keep in very frequent telephonic touch — are amazed by our similar characteristics and reactions to people and events. We have reached that wonderfully comfortable stage at which we exchange and take each other's constructive advice as well as criticism and both rely on our very special friendship.

Ann Hodges has a sister, Lorraine Lemmer, who is 10 years older than her. Both agree they had little in common as children and became closer when most sisters are growing apart. The point at which the younger sister breaks away from the 'nest' often marks growing together, of doing similar things:

I'm more like friends now with my sisters, Pam who's 31, and Shirley who's 38. The age difference doesn't seem as significant as when we were younger. When Shirley had her first son I was only 18; now I'm married, and would like children of my own. Until now I'd always been the little sister at home.

Dawn

LEFT LOOKING AFTER THE PARENT!

The youngest sister is often the one who can find herself tied by responsibility to the family home. Whereas the oldest sister took responsibility as a child, it often falls to the younger to take responsibility for an elderly parent. One woman says:

When my sister moved out of London I was the one left at home with mum who became ill. I did get resentful. I think you would have to be an angel not to. My sister didn't come up very often. I know she had her children but I think she should have made visiting mum more of a priority. But I don't think it is wise to have arguments and recriminations about it now. We'd both put forward our own views and still not solve anything.

Certainly it is times of crisis—perhaps the death of a parent—when sisters who have lived quite separate lives, pull together. Although generally a time of great sadness, the sisterly bond is at its best, rising to the fore and showing its strengths. Sisters who may not have spoken for years feel the need to get back together:

I had moved to Manchester when I married, my sister staying in London where she works. We'd long fallen out over some money I'd lent her which she never gave me back. I never really forgave her: particularly when she started earning lots in London and I was struggling to make ends meet. But when my father died everything was forgotten—it was pointless to dredge up the past. She was my sister—the only one who shared the great love we had for the same man. It made us realize how important family is, and how futile it is not to make the most of having a sister.

Kay

We only came together when both parents died within the space of a year. We'd always been great rivals for our parents' love, and were fiercely jealous of one another. That continued and was transferred on to our own children—I always wanted my parents to love my children more than Fran's, and she's told me she felt the same. But then when they died, the rivalry was no longer there, it turned into just a great loyalty to each other as sisters who both loved the same people with equal might.

Judith

Jane Thomas still finds it painful to talk about the death of her mother:

It was so important to have my sister, someone within the family who knows exactly what you're going through. You can bypass all the emotions because it goes without saying that you're both experiencing the same pain.

SOMEONE TO TALK TO

Likewise sisters often rally round if one of them has marital problems: having a sister is like having a personal marriage counsellor. When Jackie Onassis heard her younger sister, Lee, was being divorced, she flew to London to be with her, taking her to the theatre, on shopping trips and keeping her mind occupied. Earlier, when President Kennedy was shot, Lee and her husband had flown to New York, and Jackie, who clearly needed her sister, announced 'Lee will be sleeping with me in my bedroom.'

Pat Bradford remembers the very first time her younger sister came to her for advice:

Sue was very involved with her marriage and her career, and we had always lived quite independently of each other. We had become closer when we were both married, but she had never confided in me before.

The first time she came to me she told me she was thinking of leaving her husband, and she asked what I thought. In a way I felt I let her down because I didn't tell her what I think she wanted to hear. It was because I worried for her—she was in love with a man who was married with two children, and I thought he might leave her and she would be alone. She went away feeling I had not been understanding.

Sue made the right decision though, says Pat. She left her husband, remarried and was incredibly happy. Although the younger sister, it was Sue who, in turn, helped Pat through her own marriage break-up, and both supported each other when their mother was ill in hospital and later died.

Another woman was surprised by how deeply her divorce affected her sisters, especially the one closest to her in age, Teresa. Later Teresa had her own marital problems and the tables turned. For both it was important to have someone who would 'just sit' with them and 'listen'.

However, author Alexandra Connor found that when her marriage split up, she felt a split with her sister too:

When two sisters are married they have more in common. When one is divorced, she is suddenly leading a single life, has much more freedom to go back out in the world, while the married sister has security, children and her world is so much smaller. She was married with two kids, I was divorced with two careers. She was in the country, I was in the capital. We're like a coin with two faces, disparate characters, like oil and water, chalk and cheese.

In the back of my mind I'd like to think we'll come back together and that there'll be communication between us that will work. As it is she's never commented on my books and paintings, and I think for us to get together now would only be if one of us was in need of help or wanted to crow about success. So I'm not going to force it, but I think it will happen.

On the surface you couldn't get a better example of disparate lifestyles than that of Margaret Thatcher and older sister, Muriel Cullen. Whereas Mrs Thatcher wakes up at No. 10, and spends her days in meetings with other world leaders deciding on nuclear arms and monetary policy, her sister Muriel rises early at her farmhouse near Harwich, Essex and sets to work with husband Billy, running their many acres of land. Different no doubt, but both sisters are hard-working, staunch Conservatives, happily married and successful in their own right. It has been said that Mrs Thatcher knows sister Muriel is firmly behind her.

DIFFERENT OPINIONS

Fortunately Margaret Thatcher and Muriel Cullen support the same party, as politics have been seen to cause sisterly rifts.

Religious beliefs, too, can be breeding grounds for bitterness. Eliz-

Margaret Thatcher and her elder sister Muriel Cullen. (Courtesy Camera Press).

abeth I and her half sister Mary were the children of Henry VIII and for some time lived together at Hatfield, under the care of Lady Shelton, Elizabeth's aunt on her mother's side. It was not a happy time for Mary and, unlike Elizabeth, she was to suffer from their father's ruthless streak. Although he had originally been proud of his first daughter he could not forgive her for her dedication to her mother's faith—Roman Catholicism. However, half-sister Elizabeth always refused to engage in plots against Mary, despite their differing faiths.

The Second World War caused the only serious rift in the Mitford family.

Unity and Jessica were great friends in their teens, but Unity became dedicated to fascism, while Jessica found her loyalties were with communism. Before the war they turned a huge sitting room at the top of the family home into a divided drawing room where their political differences were acted out: Unity's side had fascist insignia, photographs of Mussolini, and the swastika; while Jessica's had a small bust of Lenin which she had bought in an old bookshop for a shilling. In *Hons and Rebels* she writes: 'Sometimes we would barricade with chairs and stage pitched battles, throwing books and records until Nanny came to tell us to stop the noise.' But as the rift became deeper Jessica wrote of her fears of possibly 'losing' the sister she loved:

> I still loved Boud for her huge glittering personality, for her rare brand of eccentricity, for a kind of loyalty to me which she preserved in spite of our now very real differences of outlook. When I thought about it, I had a sad and uneasy feeling that we were somehow being swept apart by a huge tidal wave over which we had no control.

Two days after war broke out, Unity, distraught that the two countries she loved most should be at war, shot herself and was badly wounded. She survived but spent years of ill health with her parents. Jessica wrote that she 'mourned my Boud of Boudledidge days, my huge bright adversary . . . when we used to fight . . . under the banners of swastika and hammer and sickle!'

WE DON'T SEE MUCH OF EACH OTHER BUT. . .

For sisters brought up within the same family their early closeness cannot be forgotten as differing beliefs and lifestyles develop or distance comes between them. A recent example is that of Sarah, Duchess of York. Her elder sister Jane lives with her husband in a remote Australian farmhouse, taking care of her two children, hundreds of cattle and sheep, and thousands of acres of wheat. In the Australian magazine *Woman's Day*, she says that despite their different lifestyles they couldn't be more close: 'There was only Sarah and I so we did things together. She's tremendous, I miss her.' But the telephone has become a vital link between them and helped to lessen the miles that keep the girls apart.

Jane remembers how 'an hour before the engagement was announced Sarah phoned to share the news with me'. And at the wedding who was one of the page boys? Jane's son Seamus, of course.

Similarly Laraine Ashton, who runs one of London's top model agencies, will often try to get a line to her sister, who now lives in Venezuala:

Jane and Sarah with their father, Ron Ferguson. (Courtesy Camera Press).

She's been living there for a number of years, and I still miss her like mad. I wish we could spend more time together, but we phone each other all the time. We talk about absolutely anything and we're always very honest with each other, and I instinctively know when she's feeling unhappy. We're a very close family and I think our closeness as sisters has a lot to do with the way we were brought up. I cherish close family ties, and, although we fought like cat and dog when we were younger, I always felt very passionately about her.

Australian sisters Lynne and Dale Spender have become known as the 'scribbling sisters', which became the title of a book containing their almost daily letters to one another.

Lynne was in Australia and Dale living in London when their letter writing really got going. In one of the earliest letters Dale wrote:

I miss you, I still haven't adjusted to your absence and have gone to speak to you on more than one occasion. I feel silly when I realize that you are 12,000 miles away and unlikely to answer.

Both sisters derive great pleasure from writing to one another:

We know it takes time, but probably not as much time as we would undoubtedly spend in each other's company if we were both living in the same city.

The invisible chain keeps its sisters linked together. Indeed, the potential forces of politics, religion, distance and men, have a fair battle on their hands when it comes to challenging sisterhood.

Chapter 6

SISTERS ARE FOR LIFE

<u>CAN RIFTS BETWEEN SISTERS BE HEALED? DO PRESENT DAY SISTERS</u>
<u>MISS OUT BY NOT MAKING THE MOST OF THEIR RELATIONSHIP?</u>

No-one can dispute the fact that sisterhood is the most long-lasting of all relationships. Sisters are sisters for life—you can't get a divorce, even if at times you might have wanted to!

An invisible bond does exist, which carries sisters through all amounts of changes and trauma. Often it's a situation of accepting the changes and carrying on:

> Although we lived separate lives and have all gone our separate ways, live miles apart, when we get together it's as if it's yesterday when we last saw each other. It's not like the old days when you moved away and that was it—you had to accept that it was too far by horse and cart to get back. I always said to my mum, the more places her daughters move around the globe, the more faraway holidays she could have!
>
> *Lucy*

As sisters grow older they change and so does their relationship.

> I think our relationship has changed a great deal from when we were growing up in Maida Vale. I think our roles have reversed— she used to be the bossy, independent one, and I think I'm more independent now. I have been on my own for a long time now.

I never wanted to marry and have children, whereas she did. I think it happens that when independent people marry and have children they change because all their efforts go towards supporting their children, and she's tended to follow the lead of her husband.

We're quite different people now: I'd been looking after Mum who was a total invalid and, when she died, Joan thought I was going to be desperately lonely, and said I should get someone to share my flat. But I knew I liked being able to do what I wanted when I wanted and I do not mind living on my own, although I like the feeling that people are living around me. Joan hates to be solitary. She and her husband said I could go and live with them but I don't know if that would work. I've been independent for a long time, and I think as we get older neither of us would want to give up our own lifestyles to live together. When I was younger I never objected to things, but now I'm more strong minded . . . Sometimes I still feel she's playing up the older sister bit, even though I'm 63! Like when I am driving with her in the passenger seat, I always feel edgy that she's watching me and start driving badly.

Joan was always my big sister and I was her kid sister and I think she still thinks of me in that way.

Sylvia

Another sister, now 55, says:

I think even when I'm drawing my pension, my sisters will always think of me as the young one. Although I'm married and have children of my own I'm still the baby of the family!

Alice

CARE AND CARE ALIKE

Ivy, the oldest of five sisters, took on the role of mother to her youngest sister, Amy. There were 14 years between them, and Ivy—still a schoolgirl—would rush home after class to help wash and feed her. Now Ivy is in her seventies and it is 59-year-old Amy who is taking care of her eldest sister:

Ivy loves talking about the old days and how she would dress me up and take me to the park. It seems strange that she now lives with me and my family and I cook her meals and take care of her. To my children, she has been a 'grandmother' figure just as she was a 'mother' figure to me.

Pat Bradford, 49, experienced a reversal of roles when her younger sister Sue, who died in 1987, became ill with cancer:

> Although she was eight years younger than me she was always the more positive, decisive one. When she became ill our roles reversed and I had to be the strong one. She was ill for two years, and I think that was the first time she really depended on me. In the last few months her husband Philip and I cared for her at home and I think all three of us needed each other.
>
> When Sue died I felt it should have been me—she was the youngest and such a vital person. Philip has told me that if anything happened to him he would like me to be legal guardian to their two sons. I'm not a natural maternal 'mumsy' type but I love those boys as my own. It seems so unfair that Sue isn't here to see them.
>
> Sue was my dearest friend and I don't think a day goes by when I don't think of her.

Before she died, Sue wrote of her sister:

> Our closeness has increased with crisis, recently my own illness. I have come to rely on my husband and Pat for support and love and I don't know what I would have done without them. Pat is an unusually special person, much loved by all her friends and family and I feel very lucky that she is my sister and that we have grown so much closer over the years. I can't imagine a time when we wouldn't be close and love each other.

WE'VE SHARED SO MUCH

Sisters have spoken about how their roles have been reversed in crisis. It seems something similar happens when a sister dies. The remaining sister has been known to take on their role and often their ambitions, too. This is particularly true of twins, or very close sisters who have always seen themselves as part of a 'pair'. As the sole survivor of this partnership, they become the 'total' person, adopting characteristics and sometimes lifestyles which were once the province of a sibling:

> When Val died I was devastated. But as the months passed I felt a sense of freedom to explore the parts of life which had been 'hers'. She had always been the organizer, and I'd been happy to fall in with her plans, but everyone's said they've seen this complete personality change and *I'm* the one making plans for everyone else. Either I was a born organizer, stifled by my older sister's

personality, or I've picked up on her characteristics to compensate for the loss.

It would be unfair to claim it's one way or the other—sisterhood is anything but predictable. But in one area there is general agreement: that the shared experiences and closeness of childhood and adolescence are all-important to the affection and warmth sisters feel for each other in adulthood and old age.

What happens between sisters in those early childhood years—from playing together to praying together is of real significance to people in their seventies and eighties, according to child psychologists.

Victor Cicirelli carried out a series of studies of adult siblings at all stages of life and he discovered that in middle age 68 per cent felt close or extremely close to their siblings, rising to 83 per cent in old age.

One sister remarks:

I don't think sisters have to like each other terribly much to feel a security in their love for each other. It may not be evident when you're young, but as adults it is good to know that there's someone who has a sort of obligation to you.

In old age rivalry mellows into friendship and security. Age Concern say that, despite the myths about the breakdown of the family unit, it is siblings who can provide most security in later years. Sisterhood withstands separation and provides a buffer against the insecurity of ageing, loss of parents or partners.

I'd looked after my mother at home when she was ill, and when she died I felt it didn't matter if I was around anymore. I hadn't married so it was just me. I remember telling my sister how I felt, and she said I mustn't feel like that. After all, I'd got her and her family. Deep down I know that my being here doesn't really alter their lives in any way. But even so there is a security in knowing that I have her. We don't see each other that often but we phone each other each week. When I was knocked down recently and had to have some stitches and was sent home, I rang her and she said she'd come straight away. If she were ill I'd go to her immediately, too.

Sylvia

In Quentin Bell's biography of Virginia Woolf, we learn that she was extremely supportive when her sister's son Julian was killed in the Spanish Civil War in 1937. Although she felt the loss to herself she was far more touched by Vanessa's grief. Quentin Bell writes: 'Virginia, being in

114

don, was of necessity a witness of her sister's first shocking paroxysms of grief. Thereafter she was a daily visitor at Vanessa's bedside, giving what consolation she could, trying with every device of her imagination to make Vanessa's existence bearable. While Vanessa lay in bed in what she herself called "an unreal state", it seemed to her that Virginia's voice was the only thing that kept life from coming to an end'.

If there was ever a day when she could not get to see Vanessa, she would write to her. During that time Virginia helped her like no one else could, but even so, Vanessa found it difficult to thank her. When she received Virginia's notes, she said, 'Another love letter from Virginia! When she is demonstrative I always shrink away.'

Other sisters have spoken of the difficulty in openly expressing their love or gratitude. But often it is unnecessary to do so—the security of knowing that sisterhood is a two-way relationship is sufficient. You are there to give support one day; on another to be given that support.

Another sister talks of the security in sisterhood:

> My husband died when I was 56 and it was such a shock. Although my two sisters both lived quite a long way from me they were immediately at my side. I really needed their support, and because of their similarity in ages, and because they knew me so well, they could just help with their presence and sympathy.
>
> *Florence*

Win Mitchell finds it's widowhood that has brought her closer to her two sisters again:

> We all went our separate ways and married. We each had our own friends and interests. But now, as three widows, we are back together again. My youngest sister lives next door, and I see her almost daily. The other one lives in Shrewsbury and we're regularly on the phone to each other.

GROWING CLOSER TOGETHER

The famous Macdonald sisters, whose lives are chronicled by Ina Taylor in *Victorian Sisters*, became closer as they grew older. Each of the four sisters achieved fame in their own right, or through marriage or their children.

Marriage and different lifestyles had originally pulled the Macdonald sisters apart, 'nostalgia and loneliness gradually brought them together again, as they sought in sisterhood the affection they had failed to find as married women.'

The four sisters were all devastated when their mother, Hannah, died, particularly Agnes, who became withdrawn and would only talk to Louie about childhood days. It was the closest they had been since both women had married. 'The melancholy which had been very much a part of Hannah Macdonald's nature surfaced again in her daughters as they looked back with longing on their lost childhood,' writes Ina Taylor.

Agnes wrote and told Louie how she would regularly fetch out the letters they wrote to each other in 1865 and reflect tearfully on how intimate they were in those far-off halcyon days. By 1880 much of the former rivalry had gone, to be replaced by a melancholic closeness dependent upon the past. Even Alice, separated by thousands of miles, felt a little of it now that both parents had died and her former aggression towards her sisters melted away.

Although Marje Proops and her sister Josephine don't get to see each other as much as they would like, there's unspoken security in their weekly phonecalls:

> We talk every Sunday. If I've not phoned her by 11.30 a.m. then she rings me. We have long talks—it's our time to catch up. We've grown more alike as we've got older, in the way we look as well as our personalities, and Jo is often mistaken for me. Now we're older we're not as concerned with being different as we were when younger.

Sue Cormack, now 42, sees the relationship with her older sister still developing:

> We see each other at least once a week and sometimes twice. Our father lives in supervised accommodation and we share equally visits by him to each of our homes for weekends and holidays.

Stella Greene, 45, has one older sister with whom her early relationship was 'argumentative':

> Now she is a real friend. There is no jealousy, and we've become closer through caring for our mother who is not well. We see each other once a week, perhaps twice if she 'pops in' after going to the shops. We lead different lifestyles but it doesn't interfere with our relationship.

Anne Scott is an observer of how the relationship between her two younger sisters has developed with age:

> Lily was always able to stand on her own two feet, whereas Margaret was very much the baby of the family. Even now, Lily organized

for her to move into a flat close by, so that she can help Margaret with her husband, who is unwell. Lily also takes Margaret and her husband away every year for a week's holiday.

Anne lives 70 miles from Lily and Margaret, and although she'd like to be closer, she feels she's grown too independent to regain their original closeness:

I remember when Mary, our eldest sister who's 66 now, came from the States a few years back. We had not seen each other for 36 years, and she wondered where all the closeness had gone between us. We'd all grown up, gone our separate ways, but now I think we'll be closer again, though not in the same way as we were when we were children.

Another woman comments:

Now I look back and wish we'd been closer. As you get older I think you reflect more on how things might have been. But my sister and I never got on when we lived at home and we've never really tried since. Perhaps we've both been too satisfied with our own lives to bother working at the relationship. I suppose if we'd had no-one else we'd have tried that much harder to get on. I've never needed her, nor she me. I think it would be nice to get to know her better now, but at 65 it seems a bit late to start getting to know your own sister.

It should never be too late, according to a social worker who works with elderly people in East Kent. She is witness to many women who live quite isolated existences—and it is often much later in life that sisterhood can play a vital role. In particular, she visits two elderly sisters who live ten minutes from each other but refuse to visit one another because their husbands fell out in the 1970s. She is determined to bring them together, if only for a brief visit, because she is sure they will get so much pleasure from reliving earlier days. 'They both talk of their childhood with special affection, and they are always talking to me about each other,' she says. 'I sense they feel secure knowing they are not alone, they are not the last of the family.'

It's certainly not uncommon to find sisters living together again in old age. When Marjorie and Elizabeth both lost their husbands and their children all had families of their own, it seemed a natural step for them to return to their old family ties:

Elizabeth now lives with me at Windsor and we get along superbly. She knows all my faults and foibles and we know all the little things about each other's strange ways. She knows how I like my eggs boiled, and I know how fussy she is over Timmy, her poodle. We would drive other people crazy I'm sure.

Although we never saw that much of each other or phoned regularly when we were both married, we've grown together as we've got older. I think it's a kind of closeness and awareness that exists solely because you've shared so much for so many years. Your background is a firm link, the perfect foundation.

LOSING YOUR SISTER

Nor surprisingly, that foundation is shaken by serious illness and death. Several older women who spoke about losing a sister said it was one of the most traumatic times in their lives, comparable with, if not worse than, the loss of a partner. It appears to help when there is another sister with whom to share the grief, in the same way that an only child suffers in isolation when a parent dies.

In the course of her research for *How Twins Grow Up*, Mary Rosambeau spoke to one elderly woman who wrote of her sister's death: 'It is very hard to live without her—almost impossible emotionally—and very lonely.' She describes the loss of a twin or close sibling as 'draughty down one side', which Mary Rosambeau says is a 'beautiful expression of grief', which would apply to the death of a well-loved sister, not just a twin.

The loss is often that much greater when elderly sisters, like Marjorie and Elizabeth, have lived together in later years and have come to depend on one another. If one sister dies, or is taken in to hospital, the other is left to live alone, and it can be a very lonely time.

I think I fell back on Lou when everyone else had gone. She did the same with me and neither of us resented it anyway. My husband had died in 1976, and my daughter went to live in America, so there was no one but Lou. When she was taken in to hospital I visited regularly, and it gave me something positive to do. I was completely unprepared for when she died, although I knew it was only a matter of time. Worst of all, I had no one to turn to. With Jim, my husband, I'd had Lou; when Mary went to America I had Lou; when our parents died we had each other, but this time there was no one to talk to. It was the loneliest of times. When your sister dies I think it is inevitable that a part of you goes with her. Many of the women who live close by used to remark how lucky we were to have each other and I comfort myself that at least I'd had a sister. I always say to people to make the most of it.

When you're young it's easy to make friends outside the family, so a sister becomes unnecessary—an extra—or simply a nuisance. As you get older there is often a complete reversal: one woman of 72 describes her sister of 69 as 'the most essential part of my life.'

Take two elderly sisters who live as next-door-neighbours to each other. They can often be seen bickering, but watch them at other times when they go for an early morning walk or to church, and no one could possibly mistake their closeness. To be sisterless, it would seem, is to be lonely—particularly in old age. To lose a sister is traumatic—at any age.

Some sisters find it almost impossible to accept the death of a younger sister. One woman tells of her reaction:

When my younger sister was taken ill with jaundice I visited her in hospital. She was cheerful and I thought that within a few weeks she would be at home again, enjoying her garden and all the books she loved to read. She had had a hard life, bringing up a family of four children on her own. She had had to go out to work to support them and then, in later life, she married again and looked as though she was set to enjoy the loving companionship of her husband, free from the cares of work and bringing up a family.

When her husband told me that, in spite of her seeming to be quite well in herself she would not recover and that it was only a matter of time before she died, I couldn't believe it. I kept thinking there must be some hope for her. Surely they had made a mistake?

I carried on visiting her. Her son in the Navy was flown home from abroad on compassionate leave—although my sister didn't know it was 'special' leave—and then I came to realize that she was really very ill and in a few weeks she died.

I couldn't take it in—she was my baby sister—how could it happen to her? She always visited me at least once a week later in her life and we would catch up on family gossip and laugh and share memories of the old days together. It's funny, but when you have a sister she can always remember something in the past that you'd completely forgotten, or, in the case of some family skeleton in the cupboard, perhaps never known before!

My older sister was a comfort to me. She was a widow and had had her fair share of worries and anxieties in her life. She was somehow more resigned and accepted Lily's fate. She told me, 'It is a happy release for her; she would only have had to endure lots of suffering. It's God's will.' Looking back, I don't know how my life would have been without my sisters. I had brothers, too, and they were very important to me, but as I got older it was my sisters who meant so much to me.

So is sisterhood much more special than brotherhood? Certainly the sisters who spoke of their feelings felt that the bond between them was a very special one and that women enjoy the closeness of a sibling relationship much more than men do. This is interesting when you look at research done by the National Child Development Study. They studied 11,000 children born in 1958 and noted that it is characteristic of women to prefer 'close social interaction' and that they are more likely to enjoy a close relationship.

One woman says:

My husband has two brothers—no sisters—and I always imagined that he would feel as close to them as I do to my sister—not in the same way of course, not shopping for clothes and so on, but meeting up for a soccer match or playing squash, perhaps. But although all three brothers are sport-mad they don't do things together, and apart from casually meeting up at their parents' home they don't really see one another at all.

I found this very strange and when I spoke to my husband about it he said that brothers were different to sisters, and I suppose he's right! There certainly isn't the bond that binds Cheryl and I together.

I suppose the domestic side of our lives also serves to hold us together; we have shared interests because of it. I like to think we shall always be close, always there for one another. And I feel sorry for my husband and his brothers. Although they all get on well together, now that they are married their bond has broken—if it ever existed.

GLAD TO HAVE EACH OTHER

For older women a sister is someone to share worries as much as memories. Lynne Spender wrote to her sister Dale about how lucky they are to have each other:

Does age ever worry you? Can't say it worries me now . . . Like you . . . I have a security that sisterless women don't often have. I assure you that when we retire, while I may mock you for your tendency to snore and you may chide me for my puritanism, neither of us will reject the other because of wrinkles or sagging breasts!

120

Writer Deborach Moggach sums it up thus:

> Whatever you do they will love you; even if they don't love you they are connected to you till you die. You can be boring and tedious with sisters, whereas you have to put on a good face with friends. In one word the most important thing is *familiarity*. A past no-one else knows about. It's a secret world. Just one word between Alex and myself—a word that means nothing to anyone else—and it sums up a whole period of our life. You keep your past by having sisters. As you get older they're the only ones who don't get bored if you talk about your memories. It's like when you meet someone who's been to India, and you have too; you can talk for hours. Everyone else around you is bored but you're totally enthralled by each other's words. It's like that with sisters.

Matilda and Harriet Thorpe love talking about their happy childhood:

> We had a wonderful time. Our mum was a film writer and when I was five she went to write Hollywood movies and she took us both out with dad. It was extraordinary. We used to play on the back lot of 20th Century Fox and Paramount, and we knew all the stars. I've been told that when I was seven, I had an ice cream sitting on Warren Beatty's knee! We were over there for 15 years in all and we're sure we're now so close because of all those extraordinary experiences we've shared.

In *The Mitford Family Album*, Sophia Murphy, daughter of one of the Mitford sisters says, 'With all the sisters, reminiscing plays a part in every conversation. Almost any subject under discussion would remind one of them of something that happened in the past, which would be recounted with shrieks of laughter!'

The secret language, once shared, still applies in old age.

The Beverley Sisters have always been a model of sisterly love. As they've got older the closeness has not lessened.

In 1985, they made a pretty spectacular comeback at the Hippodrome in London, later re-recording a 'disco' version of their hit record *Sisters*. About the same time they pooled their resources to buy a plot of land in Totteridge, North London, where three identical red brick houses were built side by side. In one lives Joy and her husband, another houses Babs and Teddie, and number three is for the sisters' three singing daughters, The Foxes, who have yet to repeat the success of their mothers.

The three 'first generation' sisters still share many common interests, 'like knitting and gardening and visiting each other'. Fortunately they don't have far to go now! 'We have never split up because blood is thicker than water,' Babs once said. 'We have our disagreements, and whoever feels strongest wins. We all get a turn at winning.'

ETERNAL RIVALS

We've seen that many sisters never achieve closeness to this degree at any point during their relationship but fortunately few have experienced such long-time rivalry as that which existed between Olivia de Havilland and Joan Fontaine. Even at a much older age, Joan says she could never look at a statue of Christ on the crucifix without her early anguishes returning to her of the time when Olivia would read aloud 'the crucifixion from the Bible in mounting gusto. I not only experienced man's inhumanity to man, but that of sister to sister.'

The childhood memories came flooding back when Joan was the first of the two sisters to win an Oscar. She remembers Olivia, who was sitting directly opposite her, ordering, 'Get up there, get up there!'

All the animus we'd felt about each other as children, the hair pullings, the savage wrestling matches, the time Olivia fractured my collar bone, all came rushing back in kaleidoscope imagery. My paralysis was total. I felt Olivia would spring across the table and grab me by my hair. I felt aged four, being confronted by my older sister . . . It was a bittersweet moment. I was appalled that I'd won over my sister.

In later years, Joan Fontaine still felt the continuing rivalry of the 'first' in her relationship with Olivia, and she later joked about being the first one to die.

PUTTING ALL THAT BEHIND YOU

Although Olivia and Joan dispute the theory, the good news for sisters in not so happy relationships is that in most cases they improve with age! Singer Sinitta is hopeful that her relationship with her sister will improve given time:

I think we're going to need each other in the future, and I've told her that we've got to sort something out.

Sadly, Jayne Irving has not had the opportunity to develop the relationship with her two sisters, born with Down's syndrome:

Cathy is pretty bad—she doesn't recognize me when I go to see her in Sheffield. She has got worse; she used to be able to speak a few words when she was younger. In fact, Helen had moved to Sheffield a couple of years before she died, but Cathy and she were never aware that they were sisters, which was very sad. When I see Cathy now I chat to her like a sister, and hope it is getting through to her. She is very affectionate sometimes, but she doesn't recognize me at all. I have hidden my feelings about it as I was growing up and I found it very difficult to watch documentaries about mental handicap and Down's syndrome. I haven't really completely sorted it out. I do feel this powerful emotional attachment to them and a tremendous sense of guilt. It's too late to help Helen but I've tried to get people talking about Down's syndrome on the television and want to help as much as I can.

Other sisters have spoken about how they became the caring, sharing sisters later in life, which everyone had expected of them so much earlier:

We are much more relaxed in each other's company, and we're no longer shy to say how we feel about each other. Before now we lived under the threat of each other doing better. At our age it doesn't matter any more! We do regret the years we missed when we could have been much closer, but at least my daughters have learnt by my example. They say they're determined not to lose one year of sisterhood.

Each year, as we've seen in each chapter of the book, sees changes in the sisterly relationship. From playful childhood rivalry to teenage hang-ups, ambitions differ and lifestyles change. One woman says:

When we look back we're amazed sometimes that we're still on speaking terms. We've done it all—we've hated each other and loved each other—and we're always very upfront with our emotions!

At school we were great friends, as teenagers we despised everything the other stood for, in our twenties and thirties we couldn't understand each other, in our forties we couldn't be bothered, but now we really want to be friends again. With a sister it doesn't matter how many changes you've been through, because at the end of the day you're sisters and you'll always have something which makes you very much alike.

Another woman says she remembers her whole life in the context of sisterhood, and her own happiness or misery was always as a result of something instigated by her sister:

My first memory of Mary was of a very pretty baby—too pretty for my liking! But she took a liking to me and ever since then her moods were always linked with mine. When she was excited about something (like when she heard she'd got a job in London) I was swept along by her enthusiasm. When she was down, I was pulled down, too. For a long while I lived my life through her, but as she became more independent so did I. I'm 68 now and she moved in with me two years ago and suddenly it's like I've got two lives again: hers and mine. Life would certainly not be as interesting without a sister.

Violet Parsons, in her 86th year, has many years of sisterhood to look back on. Her childhood days were spent in Peckham with her sisters and brother. She was the eldest:

I weighed one-and-a-half pounds when I was born and the doctor told my grandmother, who had delivered me, 'She won't live more than an hour, so don't worry about finding clothes for her,' but I did live!

My mother said I used to be wrapped in cotton wool until I grew into the smallest sized baby clothes! No special incubators for under-sized babies in those days!

My sister Dorrie came after me. She was four-and-a-half years younger, and then came Win, a year later. There was just the three girls until my brother Ralph was born much later.

Violet recalls that she used to take her two younger sisters along the path by the side of the canal to Peckham:

We would set out with a lunch of bread and dripping, or bread and jam, and a bottle of water, and have a picnic on the Rye. As soon as we got there we would sit and eat our lunch and drink the water, so that we didn't have to carry it about with us. We used to be starving and thirsty by the time we reached home again! We used to have a penny to spend between us—a halfpenny for me as the eldest and a halfpenny between the other two.

As we grew up and left school at 14 to go out to work, we made our own friends and did not go out with each other very often, but we still had to share a bedroom. There were always arguments in the morning over hair pins. The last one to do her hair would find the others had used all the pins and wouldn't have any to pin up her hair!

I was the first to marry and my sisters, and their husbands when they had married, would come and have tea with us on Sundays. Dorrie used to make such a fuss of my baby; she was married for several years before she had her daughter.

The war came and the sisters were scattered across the country.

> Of course, we did not see anything of one another then. We were all pre-occupied with our families, and the war didn't make it easy to visit one another.

It was in later years again that Violet and her sisters became closer. When Violet was the first to be widowed it was Dorrie and her husband who came to support and comfort her.

> Brian—my son—did everything he could for me and I used to go and spend one weekend with him and his family, and the next weekend Dorrie and Harry would have me to stay with them. They were very kind to me. It meant so much to me.
>
> My other sister, Win, was living at Broadstairs and used to invite me to go and stay with her and her husband, but somehow I couldn't get myself organized to travel down there from London. Feeling as low as I did, the thought of the journey was too much. Dorrie and Harry lived at Epsom and they would come in the car and take me to their home.
>
> Throughout all this time I always knew that there was 'family' to rely on, apart from my son; my sisters and my brother were always at the end of the phone if I needed them, and they would often ring and ask how I was.
>
> We were much closer in our later years. I suppose it is the 'tie' that comes with being part of a family. Both of my sisters have now died, but to have been part of a close family still gives me this sense of belonging.

Old age can bring about the break-up of sisterhood, but on the other hand, it is often easier to recognize its importance and to talk about the sisterly bond with a new awareness. Once recognized, the ties of sisterhood can have strength over everything else.

The four Hindley sisters say it's pretty tough for outsiders when they all get together because as a team they're a 'formidable force'! Says the youngest, Alison:

> We've even been known to link arms walking down the street and burst into a round of 'Sisters, sisters, there were never such devoted sisters'!

You have been warned: when sisters get together the rest of the world had better watch out!

BIBLIOGRAPHY

Quentin Bell, *Virginia Woolf: A biography* (The Hogarth Press, 1972).
Phyllis Bentley, *The Brontës and their World* (Thames and Hudson, 1986).
Elizabeth Berridge, *The Barretts at Hope End* (John Murray, 1974).
Pat Booth, *The Sisters* (Century Hutchinson, 1987).
Stephanie Calman, *Gentlemen Prefer My Sister* (Heinemann, 1984).
Celia Clear, *Royal Children from 1840 to 1980* (Arthur Barker, 1981).
Joan Collins, *Past imperfect: an autobiography* (W. H. Allen, 1984).
Marion Crawford, *The Little Princesses* (Odhams, 1950).
Nigel Dempster, *HRH The Princess Margaret: A Life Unfulfilled* (Quartet Books, 1981).
Anita Dobson, *My East End* (Pavilion, 1987).
Margaret Drabble, *Jerusalem the Golden* (Weidenfeld and Nicolson 1985).
Maureen Dunbar, *Catherine* (Penguin, 1988).
Judy Dunn, *Sisters and Brothers* (Fontana, 1984).
Simone de Beauvoir, *Memoirs of a Dutiful Daughter* (André Deutsch, 1959).
Daphne du Maurier, *Myself When Young* (Victor Gollancz, 1977).
Elizabeth Fischel, *Sisters*
Joan Fontaine, *No Bed of Roses* (W. H. Allen, 1978).
Willi Frischauer, *Jackie* (Rainbird, 1976).
Sarah Keays, *A Question of Judgement* (Quintessential Press, 1985).
Robert Levine, *Joan Collins* (Weidenfeld and Nicolson, 1985).
Judith Michael, *Deceptions* (Piatkus, 1985).
Jessica Mitford, *Hons and Rebels* (Victor Gollancz, 1960).
Janet Morgan, *Agatha Christie* (Fontana, 1984).

Patricia Murphy, *Margaret Thatcher* (W. H. Allen, 1980).

Sophia Murphy, *The Mitford Family Album* (Sidgwick and Jackson, 1985).

Gwen Robyns, *Princess Grace* (W. H. Allen, 1982).

Mary Rosambeau, *How Twins Grow Up* (The Bodley Head, 1987).

Sidney Sheldon, *Master of the Game* (Collins, 1983).

Dale and Lynne Spender, *Scribbling Sisters* (Camden Press, 1986).

Ina Taylor, *Victorian Sisters* (Weidenfeld and Nicolson, 1987).

Twiggy, *Twiggy* (Hart-Davis, MacGibbon, 1975).

Helen van Slyke, *Sisters and Strangers* (Heinemann, 1979).

Marjorie Wallace, *The Silent Twins* (Chatto and Windus, 1986 and Penguin, 1988).

Christopher Warwick, *Princess Margaret* (Weidenfeld and Nicolson, 1983).

Virginia Woolf, *Moments of Being* (The Estate of Virginia Woolf and The Hogarth Press, 1985).

Lana Wood, *Natalie: A Memoir* (Columbus Books, 1984).

Barbara Woodhouse, *Just Barbara* (Michael Joseph, 1981).